WAGES AND SALARIES

WAGES AND SALARIES:

A Handbook for Line Managers

REVISED EDITION

By Robert E. Sibson

American Management Association, Inc.

New York

Copyright © 1967 by the American Management Association, Inc. Printed in the United States of America by Vail-Ballou Press, Inc., Binghamton, N. Y.

All rights reserved. This book may not be reproduced in whole or in part without the express permission of the Association.

Library of Congress catalog card number: 67-16559

ABOUT THE AUTHOR

ROBERT E. SIBSON is a graduate of Yale University and holds a master's degree in business administration from the Wharton School of the University of Pennsylvania.

He has been an Associate Labor Relations Consultant with Simpson and Curtin of Philadelphia, Personnel Manager of the Electronic Division and later Assistant to the Director of Industrial Relations of the Otis Elevator Company, Personnel Manager of Schick Incorporated, and Personnel Manager of the Raytheon Company's Government Equipment Division.

Since 1960, he has been President of Sibson & Company, Inc., a management consulting firm in the field of employee-employer relations.

Mr. Sibson's first book, *A Survey of Pension Planning*, was published by Commerce Clearing House in 1952. He has also written a number of articles on personnel subjects for leading journals during the past fifteen years. In addition, he has been a regular seminar leader for the American Management Association, has addressed numerous conferences, and has taught graduate courses relating to personnel subjects.

CONTENTS

Introduction   13

I. Management Opportunities in
Pay Administration   17

>Owners, Managers, and Employees—Pay Problems of the Business—Exploiting Opportunities—Need for a Formal Program—Management Approach to Pay Problems—Responsibility for Wage and Salary Administration

II. The First Step: Job Evaluation   31

>The Basic Approach—Job Analysis—Methods of Job Evaluation—Use of Job Evaluation—Questions and Answers

III. The Second Step: Pricing Job Value   61

>The Techniques and Their Purposes—Pricing the Structure: The Wage Survey—Pricing the Structure: Other Considerations—Characteristics of Traditional Structures—Explaining the Pay Structure

IV. Individual Pay Determination   78

>Methods of Setting Individual Pay: Single-Rate, Informal, and Automatic—Use of the Merit Rating Process—Salary Planning

V. Administration of the Pay Program   110

>Policies, Laws, and Collective Bargaining Agreements—Ground Rules for Pay Administration—Top

Management Control—Special Administrative Considerations

VI. Wage Incentive Plans — 145

Logic of Wage Incentive Plans—Types of Incentive Plans—Methods of Determining Work Standards—Economics of Wage Incentive Systems—Elements of a Sound Wage Incentive System—Administration of the Plan

VII. Salesmen's Compensation — 160

The Sales Job: A Definition—Salesmen's Duties—Sales Job Descriptions—Elements of Sales Compensation—Incentive Versus Base Pay—Level of Total Compensation—Determining Base Salaries—Incentive Compensation Plans—Trends in Incentive Compensation—Administration of Sales Compensation Plans

VIII. Compensation of Professional Personnel — 176

Professional Jobs: What They Are—Use of Position Description—Use of Job Evaluation—Salary Structures for Professional Employees—Administration of Professional Salaries—Special Compensation for Professionals

IX. Supervisory, Technical, and Administrative Personnel — 191

Supervisory Employees—Technical Employees—Administrative Employees

X. Salary Administration for Management — 205

The Management Group—Adapting Job Descriptions to Managers—Adapting Job Evaluation Plans—Management Salary Structure—Salary Planning for Management Positions—Salary Administration for Top Executives—Incentive Compensation Plans—Stock Options—Special Compensation for Executives

CONTENTS

XI. Fringe Benefits as Additional Compensation   230
   Extent of Fringe Benefits—Checklist of Major Fringe Benefits—Administration of Fringe Benefits

Summary: The Individual Manager's Responsibilities   247

Index   250

WAGES AND SALARIES

INTRODUCTION

THE COMPLEXITIES OF PAY ADMINISTRATION IN THE MODern business firm, and the problems which pay administration poses to management, have been widely recognized. A survey of senior executives, for instance, indicates that 214 presidents who responded consider compensation the second most difficult personnel problem, both for their companies and for themselves personally. There is every sign that the complexities and, therefore, the time and cost involved in pay administration are increasing, almost by geometric proportions, because of the increasing number and diversity of positions, the growing technology inherent in many of these positions, the phenomenon of steadily rising incomes, the different forms of compensation available, and numerous other factors.

Some sort of a wage and salary administration program cannot be avoided; for, wherever the employee-employer relationship exists, there must be a pay administration program to determine the "right price for the employee's services." Thus pay administration is a part of every enterprise's activities; and the pay administration program, whatever its form, must be regarded as one of the costs of doing business.

Significant resources, in both time and money, must be allocated to this program. The goal, of course, is to expend the resources judiciously and to get a return from them which benefits the organization. To do this, the pay program should meet the following objectives:

- Help to attract and retain the numbers and types of employees required to operate the business.
- Gain the employee acceptance of company compensation policies and practices which is necessary if employees are to work constructively and effectively.
- Play a positive role in motivating employees to perform to the best of their abilities.
- Gain acceptance of pay expenditures on the part of the firm's "public"—which may include owners, government, customers, and the general public.
- Provide opportunity for employees at every level to achieve their reasonable aspirations in a framework of equity, impartiality, and reason.
- Maintain the company in a reasonably competitive position in the product marketplace.

Much could be said about each of these objectives. At first look they may seem self-evident. In fact, they are filled with complexities and frequently involve contradictions.

The first requirement for successful pay administration is a thoughtful and realistic examination of these objectives. The second is to develop company compensation policies which make achievement of the objectives possible. Without such compensation policies, the company and its individual managers are likely to be involved in continual crises over pay questions. Even when management's actions are correct in terms of the practicalities of the moment, these crises usually involve excessive costs and, over a period of time, will probably result in confusion, inequities, and trouble.

The third requirement for pay administration programs is the use of appropriate methods and techniques. No doubt some wage and salary administrators have been preoccupied with technical excellence and cleverness of procedures. Technique itself, of course, should not be the goal. Rather, methods should be designed to effectuate compensation policies, to assist managers in solving pay problems, and generally to facilitate the achievement of company objectives.

Because each company is unique in terms of its products, its organization, its policies, its managers' backgrounds, its objectives, its economic characteristics, and many other factors, there is no one best program. To fashion the most appropriate program for a given company, the staff expert's job is to choose from many sound and workable alternatives that set of techniques which is best tailored to the individual enterprise.

Given sound policy and an appropriate set of techniques and methods, the fourth leg of sound pay administration is excellence of execution. Execution includes planning, deciding, administering, and explaining pay actions. It is the line manager who is responsible for execution and who must also in most cases undertake the planning, the deciding, the administration, and the explaining. Staff specialists may help by providing information, doing various mechanical jobs and, it is hoped, giving sound advice.

The author's purpose in the following pages is to concentrate on the information in the wage and salary field which the line manager needs to know in order to meet his responsibilities under the pay program. First of all, this handbook of wage and salary administration has been designed to provide supervisors with adequate background on policies and techniques. Secondly, the book contains material which should guide supervisors in solving problems that they actually face on a daily basis. It also presents ideas and suggestions for improving their overall performance in this area.

This concentration on the practical aspects of applying a wage and salary program should not lead managers to the conclusion that the technical aspects are unimportant. Sound wage and salary administration requires sound policy guidance, sound conception of techniques, and sound application. As pay administration continues to grow more involved, the techniques and methodology become more numerous and more complex. However, qualified specialists, either on the personnel staff or from outside consulting firms, can be called upon to provide specialized technical knowledge; the line manager's concern should be to use the techniques which are provided.

The original edition of this book was based largely on a comprehensive study of wage and salary administration in 15 leading companies; discussions with employees and line managers in Raytheon Company, Otis Elevator Company, Schick Incorporated, Armstrong Cork Company, and the Lancaster Plant of RCA; and the extensive research information at the American Management Association. Since then, experience in assisting over 100 firms in a consulting capacity has reinforced the author's convictions about much of what was reported in the original volume and has been the basis for much that has been added. More importantly than pay-level raises, new techniques of administration, new forms of computation, and an increasing focus on compensation practices for exempt-level employees warrant, and are incorporated in, this revised edition.

It would not be possible to give credit to all those who contributed to this project in both editions, because of the many sources of information. The author is particularly indebted to his associates in Sibson & Company, Inc., for this revised edition. Much of the credit, however, goes to his first partner in the company, who typed and edited the manuscript, did much research in connection with it, and is a constant collaborator and source of encouragement.

CHAPTER I

MANAGEMENT OPPORTUNITIES IN PAY ADMINISTRATION

WAGE AND SALARY ADMINISTRATION IS A MANAGEMENT method which can be valuable to the business, helpful to the manager, and at least reassuring to the employee. If it is to serve these purposes, all but the smallest enterprises must first have some formal wage and salary program. The program should be geared to the needs of the particular business, and everyone concerned should understand his responsibilities under it.

Owners, Managers, and Employees

Employee compensation represents a substantial part of the total operating costs of any business. How well the company controls these wage costs, and how much employee productivity is obtained in return for the wage dollar, can have an important effect on the success of any enterprise. For the business where wage costs are a large percent of total costs, and for the business whose products are the services of people, wage costs and productivity may be the crucial elements of success or failure.

Similarly, the success of each manager depends in part on wage costs and employee productivity in his own department. Managers are also personally concerned about salary administration because they are employees who work for a salary. This personal involvement should serve as a constant reminder, even to the most business-oriented manager, that the "price" of employee services represents income to employees, as well as part of the cost of doing business. To the employee, this price evaluates his experience and effort and determines the standard of living of his family.

The company wage and salary program is therefore important alike to employees, managers, and owners. When the objectives of the three tend to be in conflict, the program may be a means of solving pay problems in such a way as to balance the interests of each group.

Pay Problems of the Business

Although pay problems may vary considerably between different companies, and even between different departments in the same company, certain basic problem areas are common to most operations. Management recognition of these areas is the first step toward their solution.

One problem which exists in every enterprise is the question of pay relationships within the company. Comparing their pay with that received by fellow workers is not only the natural thing for employees to do but also the easiest income comparison for them to make. Where they believe they see inequities, they will tend to feel that they are underpaid, they may suspect favoritism, and they will generally lose confidence in the company pay program regardless of their actual pay level.

Employees are also sensitive about the pay received for comparable work in other companies. Their knowledge of pay elsewhere is generally imperfect, but if they get the impression that their own is lower, serious employee unrest will probably result. This problem not only is an important factor in employee attitudes but also affects the company's ability to attract and retain the number and types of persons required to operate efficiently. Moreover, since relative pay levels affect relative costs, they have a bearing on the company's ability to compete effectively in the product market.

Reward for outstanding work constitutes another important pay problem for employees and managers. People who perform more competently than others will generally expect more money in return. Unless they get it, their desire to do more efficient work will very likely be discouraged or destroyed altogether.

Finally, there is a broad range of pay problems that are essentially administrative in nature:
- Establishment of policies, procedures, and practices which help managers solve their innumerable daily pay problems and get rapid answers to problems that are outside their authority.
- Communication of pay information to supervisors and employees to promote understanding and gain reasonable acceptance of the company pay program.
- Maintenance of a proper balance among base pay, premium payments, fringe benefits, pay for time not worked, and various forms of indirect payments to employees.
- Maintenance of proper records and other data which managers need in order to make intelligent pay decisions.
- Conformity with various legal requirements.

Unless the company meets these problems realistically, it faces constant grievances and employee discontent that may result in lower productivity and greater turnover. The lowered productivity, particularly among management and professional employees, may be difficult to measure because it will not necessarily be manifested in overt reactions but may take the more subtle form of indifference, indolence, politicking, or just plain loafing. If these problems lead to high turnover, it is likely to be the company's most effective workers who leave, because they are typically more sensitive to inequities in pay and are better able to obtain positions elsewhere.

Exploiting Opportunities

Solving the pay problems of the business frequently represents a limited objective. Inherently, solutions usually involve expending time and money to avoid trouble, correct past mistakes, or meet one-time situations. Certainly the first objective of every pay program must be to avoid trouble; unfortunately, many pay programs do not even achieve this limited goal.

Often, however, there are "opportunity situations" as well as "problem situations" in wage and salary administration. Wage and salary practices can be set up so that they not only avoid trouble by eliminating problems but also will make positive contributions toward increasing employee productivity and effectiveness or achieving other goals of the business.

EXHIBIT 1
Solving Pay Problems: The Value/Cost Concept

Response to Pay Problem	Units of Time or Cost*	Units of Business Value (+) or Loss (−)*
Do nothing	0	−100
Do the wrong thing	100	−100 or −200
Solve the problem	100	0
Solve the problem and exploit an opportunity	110	+100

*Numbers are illustrative only.

As Exhibit 1 shows schematically, only incremental costs are usually involved in a wage and salary practice which exploits opportunities as well as solves problems. In a sense, the hundred units of cost are an expense of the business, for they avoid detractions from company goals. But the small incremental units of cost required to exploit an opportunity can truly be regarded as an investment—an investment which frequently yields extraordinary capital returns.

Examples of opportunity situations will be seen in specific practices described throughout this book. The point here is that, so far as management actions are concerned, it is essential not only to look at real problems but also to be constantly alert to opportunities. For, in wage and salary administration, problem solutions may avoid dissatisfaction but at the same time may not necessarily also create satisfaction.

Need for a Formal Program

The very complexity of these pay matters usually requires a reasonably formalized wage and salary program, except in the smallest operation. A formal program, though difficult to define, is characterized by the establishment of standards which serve to guide or control individual pay decisions. Such guides are "formalized" in the sense that they are predetermined and put in writing. Of course, they do not represent a substitute for human judgment, but they can contribute to more consistent, more sound, and less subjective decisions.

Just how useful a formalized approach may be depends both upon the correctness of the policies, techniques, practices, and ground rules that are established in the first place and upon the quality of the managers' decisions within this framework. A formal program does run the risk of becoming restrictive and inflexible. This can happen if it becomes an end in itself rather than a means to an end, if it is used as a staff technique rather than as a management practice, or if, as sometimes happens, it is taken as a substitute for judgment.

The usefulness of a formal program can be evaluated by comparing it with other approaches which might be followed. One alternative may be labeled the "market approach." It rests primarily on the proposition that managers need merely pay the "going rate" for workers in various categories and market forces will automatically result in equitable pay. This may have been a practical method of solving company pay problems at some time in the past, but under current conditions use of a survey as the sole means of setting pay is an unworkable approach. Labor markets are not that clearly defined, survey methods are imperfect, and many jobs are unique to the individual company. Furthermore, the application of the "natural laws of supply and demand" may be too harsh to be acceptable to employees, the business, or the community.

Individual bargaining has been found equally unacceptable as a basic approach. For one reason, the preponderance of bargaining strength almost invariably rests with the employer. For another, the application of brute strength can hardly be counted on to produce realistic solutions to pay problems. Finally, individual bargaining brings chaotic conditions in both the employment market and the company's internal pay relationships.

Collective bargaining, on the other hand, may equalize bargaining strength and eliminate favoritism, but it does not necessarily bring more logical pay decisions. Without standards to guide the thinking, control the prejudices, and restrain the arbitrary decisions of negotiators, the results of collective bargaining are no more inherently correct than the results of individual bargaining. For these reasons, negotiators in mature collective bargaining situations guide their thinking by many of the techniques normally associated with a formal wage and salary approach.

Actually, elements of the market approach, individual bargaining, and frequently collective bargaining may be a part of even the most formalized pay program. Every company is influenced to some extent by the pay received by employees of other companies. Furthermore, since formal programs are only guides to human judgment, individual bargaining plays a part in any pay program, for whenever judgment is exercised, some personal thinking and human values will be reflected in the decisions that are made. Lastly, the adoption of any formal pay program in a group of unionized employees is itself subject to collective bargaining.

Management Approach to Pay Problems

A number of techniques and procedures have been developed to guide managers' pay decisions under a formal wage and salary program. The basic elements are outlined in Exhibit 2 and will be discussed in some detail in later chapters. The important thing to recognize is that these techniques will not automatically attain the objectives indicated. Like all management techniques, they must be used properly if they are to prove genuinely helpful in solving pay problems.

Also note that each technique has been evolved as a means of meeting an actual business pay problem. This reflects a fundamental principle which should underlie wage and salary administration: Each practice, policy,

EXHIBIT 2

Elements of a Formal Wage and Salary Program

Technique Used	Objective of Technique
Job analysis	To determine job facts as a necessary step in job evaluation (as well as in employment, management development, organizational studies, and general supervision).
Job description	To record job facts.
Job evaluation	To determine relative job worth.
Job grading	To administer pay scales effectively.
Job pricing	To translate relative job worth into money values.
Incentive or merit plans	To reward employees for higher production and better job performance.
Fringe benefits	To provide economic security and "extra compensation" and to correct, control, or compensate employees for undesirable conditions of work.
Communications	To give supervisors the information they need in order to carry out the program and to gain acceptance of it.
Administrative procedures and practices	To resolve individual problems, keep the program current and operating efficiently, and provide general guidance to managers.
Union participation	To meet the requirements of collective bargaining.
Controls	To insure reasonably consistent and correct application of the wage and salary program and to maintain control over costs.

procedure, or technique *should be based on actual company operating needs*. Regardless of how technically clever a wage and salary technique may be, it has no inherent value in itself.

The principle that techniques should be geared to needs suggests a basic approach to pay problems which is equally applicable to the needs of individual managers and to those of the company as a whole. This basic approach involves:

- Identifying needs.
- Determining objectives.
- Developing programs.
- Planning and executing the programs.

Identifying needs. The first step in this approach to wage and salary administration is a realistic appraisal of needs. Too frequently company needs are assumed to be self-evident. Defining them is seldom this simple, however, and it is easy to be misled by casual observation, by preconceived notions, or by opinions based upon incomplete knowledge of important facts.

Needs can be determined in various ways. Personnel specialists should have sufficient knowledge and experience to predict problems and to spot problem symptoms. Staff should also be able to help identify needs by knowing the right questions to ask—an ability which can sometimes be as valuable as knowing alternative answers. In addition, available payroll data, grievance records, reports of exit interviews or opinion surveys, and other company material can be useful in identifying needs. A great deal can be learned by talking directly with employees; in this way, management can at least learn what pay problems exist in their minds. Finally, line managers themselves have knowledge of the company's pay problems from their operating experience.

Determining objectives. It may not be practical to attempt to solve all the pay problems which can be identified. Some of them, such as the intrusion of personal judgment in pay decisions, cannot be solved by any known method. Others which appear on the surface to be pay problems may actually involve organizational planning, work scheduling, manpower planning, or recruitment. Too, the solution of one pay problem may create other more serious ones, or the time and effort involved may be prohibitive. Because of such considerations, it is important to make a qualitative analysis of needs and then to translate these needs into realistic, specific, and attainable objectives.

Developing programs. After objectives have been established, it is possible to consider various techniques and procedures for achieving them. The approach which calls for determining needs, setting objectives, and then designing programs may seem laborious, but it does not involve more effort in the long run. Only in this way is it possible to insure that the resulting programs are genuinely geared to actual problems. Furthermore, pay programs are easier to design and apply when the preliminary steps of determining needs and objectives are done well.

Planning and executing the programs. Once a program is determined, there must be some planning of the manner in which it will be carried out. Unless this is done, important aspects of it may not be accomplished, indecision and confusion will probably result, and there is certain to be considerable inefficiency. It is also important to establish a timetable since this helps to insure that the various operations will be performed in the correct sequence and that the work will be finished on time. A timetable also sets a goal for those who have responsibilities under the program. In addition, planning should provide for follow-up at various stages to determine both progress and results. Finally, it is important to specify who is responsible for accomplishing the various aspects of the program that has been established.

Responsibility for Wage and Salary Administration

Responsibility should be fixed carefully so that each person who is associated with the program knows exactly what is expected of him. The question is basically one of determining which assignments will be given to the individual supervisor, which will be retained by higher-level line management, and which will be assigned to staff personnel.

There can be little quarrel, of course, with the proposition that the individual line manager must retain the basic authority and responsibility for the pay of his subordinates. So long as pay actions can be properly regarded as instruments of reward, incentive, and corrective discipline, the individual manager must be responsible for them if he is to be responsible for the performance of his subordinates. Furthermore, he is held accountable for costs in his group, and he must therefore have responsibility for the very important element of wage costs.

Limitations by top management. In actual practice, however, the individual manager seldom has complete authority and responsibility for wage and salary administration. His authority must be limited by higher-level managers for various reasons—for example, the need for consistency in administering the wage and salary program among the different sections of the company. Thus policy formulation is generally retained by top management. Higher-level management may also limit the authority of individual managers by establishing techniques and procedures to insure conformity with company policies. Furthermore, top management must recognize that wage and salary administration encompasses a considerable body of knowledge and skill. It would be both unreasonable and impractical to expect all line managers to become expert in this specialized field.

Functions of the line manager. Line managers have the basic responsibility for making pay decisions within the framework of policies, practices, and techniques which have been established by the company. The quality of their day-to-day decisions is really the heart of any wage and salary program.

Frequently, line managers also have a role to play in policy formulation. Even where they do not participate in it on a formal basis, they are responsible for supplying information relating to operating needs and experiences, as well as any constructive ideas for improved wage and salary administration.

Invariably the individual manager is involved in policy interpretation and application. Policies represent general statements of intent on the part of the company, and they are established primarily to guide the thinking of management throughout the organization. In applying them, line managers are spelling out what these policies really mean. Since each interpretation becomes a precedent which will have a bearing upon future interpretations, in a sense this function of individual supervisors is a part of policy making.

Consequently each manager should exercise considerable care in applying policy. Although every problem he faces has unique aspects, he should consider the following basic questions in relation to it:
 1. What are the company policies on this question?
 2. Do I know the important facts and circumstances necessary to answer it?
 3. How did I previously handle a similar problem?
 4. Should I discuss the question with the wage and

salary staff in order to gain a better understanding of company policy, to benefit by their broader experience, or to see how similar questions have been handled in other sections of the company?
5. Should I consult my immediate supervisor before reaching a decision?
6. Is the union involved? If so, should I discuss the matter with the union steward or the labor relations staff?
7. Should I tell my other subordinates about the decision?
8. How am I going to explain my decision to the employee or employees who raised the question in the first place?

Ideally, it should be an objective for each supervisor to gain employee acceptance of the company wage and salary program. The supervisor is not likely to gain that acceptance unless employees understand the company pay policies and practices. Clearly, the basic responsibility for explaining these rests with him because he can take advantage of the various daily questions and problems to do it. It goes without saying, of course, that he cannot explain the program to employees unless he understands it himself.

Staff functions. Wage and salary staff specialists also have certain areas of responsibility in carrying out the program. While the individual line manager may not be directly concerned with these areas, it is important that he have some knowledge of the staff's role in order to understand his own share in the program better.

Research in wage and salary administration is a basic staff function. It generally includes such assignments as compensation surveys; preparation of reports; administration of company controls; investigation of programs, practices, and techniques used by other companies; analysis of internal wage facts; and the development of the data that managers need in order to make logical pay decisions.

This research function of the staff is really the basis for most of the group's other duties. Because of the specialized knowledge obtained through research, the staff specialist can play a significant role in such areas as these: developing and recommending wage and salary policies, plans, programs, and procedures; assisting line managers at all levels in interpreting and applying wage and salary programs; advising and counseling line managers on the various wage and salary problems which may arise.

There are also a number of duties which are frequently assigned to staff personnel in order to gain the efficiency which results from specialization. A good example is the preparation of job descriptions. Although line supervisors can carry out this function, and do so in many companies, the actual writing of job descriptions is a time-consuming job. Having staff analysts write them may speed the entire process.

A final function of the staff lies in the area of audit and control. Top management must establish some means of auditing and controlling the wage and salary actions of managers throughout the company, and staff members are frequently used to provide this control because of their know-how, their participation in policy formulation, and their broad company views.

Auditing the performance of management can, of course, be a highly unpopular undertaking. When the same group which is supposed to advise and constructively influence line supervisors also plays a role in auditing, a delicate situation is created which requires considerable tact and understanding on the part of all concerned. What everyone must realize is that staff is not controlling, but merely performing administrative chores so that higher-level management can effectively control the program.

CHAPTER II

THE FIRST STEP: JOB EVALUATION

SOME FORM OF JOB EVALUATION IS ALMOST INVARIABLY part of a wage and salary program. A company may have many objectives in creating a job evaluation plan, but certainly the basic purpose is to establish equitable internal pay relationships. The experience of thousands of companies has shown the effectiveness of job evaluation in doing this. To form a successful plan, however, managers must be not only familiar with the technique but also aware of some pitfalls inherent in its use.

THE BASIC APPROACH

In spite of the somewhat bewildering number of plans in effect, there is really only one basic job evaluation approach. This approach, illustrated in Exhibit 3, calls for the *measurement of job duties against a predetermined yardstick in order to assess relative job worth.* The quantity measured is job duties. Thus the process is impersonal and has nothing to do with how well the work is performed or the ability, potential, or attitudes of employees. Duties are determined through some method of job analysis and are usually described in writing.

The evaluation plan itself, against which the job duties are measured, may be based on any predefined yardstick

EXHIBIT 3
The Job Evaluation Formula

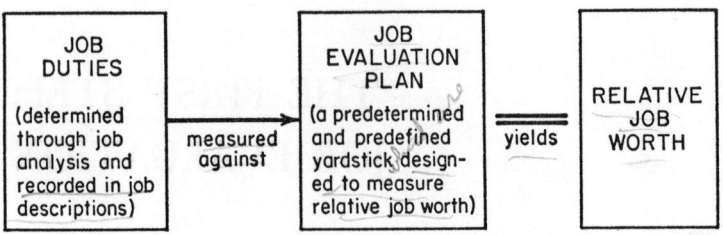

that serves to guide managers' judgments. This use of a yardstick is somewhat similar to the techniques employed by industrial engineers in establishing work standards, or those used by quality control engineers in determining inspection standards.

Job evaluation measures job worth in an administrative sense rather than an economic or social one. Economic worth can be determined only by the natural forces of supply and demand in the marketplace, social worth by the natural forces operating in such activities as individual or collective bargaining. The administrative concept of job worth involves *importance* or *difficulty*. Managers should recognize, however, that market worth, social worth, importance, and difficulty are not identical and may not always correlate perfectly. This can be one of the inherent limitations of the job evaluation process.

JOB ANALYSIS

Analysis of job duties, the first step in the evaluation process, is also the most important, because the entire evaluation program is built upon it. Job evaluation can be no more accurate than the facts upon which it is based.

What Should Be Analyzed?

The first question to be resolved before the job analysis can be undertaken is the exact meaning of the word "job." This is far more than an academic question; there are frequently much confusion and misunderstanding because of it. The five definitions below are given in order of increasing broadness:
1. "Job" means that which a person does. Under this definition, each person has a separate and distinct job, and each is reported and described separately.
2. "Job" means that which a person does or a group of persons do where the duties are the same, though perhaps not identical; they may be performed in different places, with different pieces of equipment, in different sequences, and so forth.
3. "Job" means that which a person does or a group of persons do where *most* duties are the same, and where those that are not the same are incidental to the main job and distinctly less valuable or difficult.
4. "Job" means family of jobs where duties vary but interchangeability of work is possible, and where the nature of all the work is similar.
5. "Job" means group of jobs in a common environment, where different duties are performed, but all are of equal difficulty or value.

The broader the approach in determining which "job" is to be measured, the less likely it is that the job analysis and the resulting description will accurately reflect any of the jobs included. On the other hand, the more precise the job definition used, the more detailed the descriptions will be, and the more costly the evaluation process. Very restrictive definitions can result in identifying differences without distinction.

A second basic question involved in job analysis is whether the company should measure work assigned or work actually performed. Some wage and salary experts argue that unless work performed is analyzed, the company may not give employees credit for what they are actually doing. On the other hand, analyzing performed work may imply that employees should be given latitude to assign work to themselves. It is, of course, the manager's function to assign work—a fact the job analyst should never forget. The analyst is essentially an information gatherer and reporter; it is not his prerogative to judge the logic of work assignments or to determine what assignments should be made.

Methods of Analysis

What type of information, and how much of it must be obtained in job analysis, depends upon a number of considerations: for example, whether the analysis is to be used solely for evaluation or for other purposes as well; what level of jobs is being analyzed; what type of evaluation plan will be used; and what job knowledge is held by those who are going to conduct the evaluation. Certain basic areas of information, however, are pertinent in almost all job analyses. These include:
1. Fundamental purpose of the job.
2. Work assigned or performed. This may require study of:
   a. Specific tasks.
   b. Areas of responsibility.
   c. Examples of work.
3. General importance of each job element and its relation to objectives of the operation.

4. Approximate time spent on each duty or area of responsibility.
5. Scope of the job and its impact on the operation.
6. Inherent authority (not only formal delegation, but also latitude of action) and formal or informal audits on work.
7. Working relationships—including supervision, but not restricted to it.
8. Specific methods, equipment, or techniques which must be used.
9. "Climate" of the job, including objectives and working environment.
10. Conditions under which work must be performed: physical effort, hazards, discomfort, deadlines, travel, pressure, rate of change, innovations required, and the like.

This type of information can be obtained in various ways, either by a staff analyst or by the individual line manager. One quick and inexpensive technique is the questionnaire, which can be given either to supervisors or to the employees who actually perform the jobs. If handled properly, such an approach utilizes the knowledge which those who are closest to the job have, and it also gives employees an opportunity to participate in the most essential part of the evaluation program. The cost is slight, and only a very short elapsed time is required. The job incumbent must, of course, be sufficiently articulate to share his knowledge. Also, guides in the form of glossaries, instructions, and samples are most helpful.

Direct observation of the work being performed is another method of job analysis. Some observation is usually essential if the analyst is to gain a real understanding of the job duties. Done properly, observation is usually the most precise method of analysis but also the most costly.

Valuable information can also be obtained from organizational manuals, time-study reports, former job descriptions, and systems and procedures studies, when they are available. But, in the last analysis, the individual manager is the basic source of information relating to the job duties of his subordinates.

Job Descriptions and Specifications

The information uncovered in evaluation is usually recorded in job descriptions, although analysis questionnaires can double as descriptions in smaller companies. Job descriptions should employ a direct and brief style of writing. Since the same words often carry different meanings to different people, it may avoid problems of semantics to have a few skilled writers do the actual preparation, provided these people understand the job operations under study. Useful guidance in common business language is available in the form of the various published glossaries which define frequently used terms—such as "responsibility for" and "coordinates"—not well covered in standard dictionaries.

As for the format of the descriptions, they should first name the job, using the job title which most accurately reflects the duties assigned. The description of duties should also have a simple format which facilitates understanding. Finally, it should be reasonably short, presenting only pertinent information.

In addition to compiling factual data regarding job duty assignments, analysts sometimes specify the basic requirements necessary to carry out the work, such as the requisite education and experience. When these are incorporated into job descriptions, the results are commonly referred to as job specifications. Specifications may be valuable in subsequent evaluations, but the analyst is, in essence, evaluating the job without benefit of a job evaluation plan. The usefulness of specifications thus depends upon whether he is qualified to make such judgments and how precisely and meaningfully he expresses them.

Management Use of Descriptions

In its most elementary form, management's job of "getting things done through people" might be said to have six functions:
1. Thinking through what work must be done and organizing it efficiently.
2. Staffing the organization to accomplish objectives.
3. Assigning work to individuals—communicating duties and setting standards.
4. Observing and judging how well employees are performing.
5. Improving performance through appraisal and training.
6. Rewarding employees for their performance or taking appropriate corrective action.

In this context, job analysis and, where helpful, the writing of job descriptions are inherent parts of the manager's job. Basically, he will want to make certain that all work assigned is essential and that essential tasks are grouped into jobs in the most efficient and economic manner. From the resulting descriptions he can develop specifications which, in employment, promotion, or transfer decisions, will help to insure that properly qualified persons are selected. The descriptions will also be valuable to him in showing employees what is expected of them and in making sure they understand how to do the work which has been assigned.

Moreover, the listing of assigned duties in a job description helps the manager to determine reasonable standards of performance. He can review an employee's work in terms of each of the major duties listed and judge how well the employee is meeting these standards.

Job descriptions can be useful, generally, in improving manpower utilization. Consulting his completed listings, the manager can plan to eliminate time-consuming tasks which are below the overall level of work assigned to a job. These can then be reassigned to lower-paid jobs. In addition, the manager can study duties in terms of workloads to determine approximately how many man-hours are required and, with this information, judge how many employees are really needed for each phase of the work. He should be concerned with wage costs in terms of the number of employees in each pay level as well as the correctness of the pay level itself.

Finally, job descriptions are useful as a basic management-engineering tool. They may indicate possible improvements in operating procedures by pinpointing duplication of work, by indicating a better flow of work, by suggesting better use of specialization, or by pointing out possible bottlenecks. Above all, each duty can be examined with respect to its importance to the success of the operation: Is this particular task necessary? What would happen if it were not performed? Is there some way it could be done more simply? These are the questions managers should ask about every assigned duty which is listed on a job description. Much of this analysis can be accomplished by merely studying and cross-comparing descriptions. In addition, some of the more sophisticated techniques of management engineering, such as flow charts and activity-distribution charts, can be applied.

Because job descriptions can be a major aid in management development, some companies view job analysis and description writing as a management exercise, with the primary purpose of providing information required for effective management. Descriptions which serve this purpose are more than adequate for sound job evaluation. Better management is the first purpose; job evaluation a fallout advantage. Such descriptions probably cost more to prepare than those which are designed only for job evaluation purposes. Even the latter, however, require a substantial investment; and a slight additional expenditure can result in job descriptions which not only are better guides for evaluation but also can be used to improve managers' understanding of the work for which they and their subordinates are responsible.

Should Employees See Their Job Descriptions?

Some managers do not show employees their job descriptions for fear this will cause controversy or lead people to resist any work not specifically listed. If job descriptions are well prepared, however, sharing them with the employees concerned would seem to be an essential step in using them. Certainly, there can be no harm in showing a person a list of duties he is expected to perform so long as the list is factual and accurate and so long as he recognizes that his superior may ask him to perform other tasks from time to time.

Actually, sharing job descriptions with the employees concerned can be important in gaining acceptance of the job evaluation results. Unless people are convinced that their classifications were truly determined on the basis of their own job duties, it will be difficult for them to accept the results of even the most elaborate system.

METHODS OF JOB EVALUATION

Evaluation plans which are used to translate job duties into relative job worth may take many different forms.

Their technical aspects are of primary concern to the staff manager who is responsible for recommending a plan. Supervisors, however, need to know the basic aspects of the evaluation system they use, and they can benefit from gaining a general understanding of alternative systems. They may also find it useful to employ these other techniques as supplementary methods in carrying out their own share of the work.

Essentially, the principal measuring techniques that have been devised for determining the relative worth of jobs differ from one another in three areas:
1. What is measured (the whole job or identifiable elements of it).
2. How jobs are weighted (whether or not point values are assigned to establish quantitative measures of job value).
3. How jobs are measured (against other jobs or against a predetermined yardstick).

EXHIBIT 4
METHODS OF JOB EVALUATION

1. What Is Measured?	2. How Weighted?	3. How Measured? Job Against Scale	3. How Measured? Job Against Job
Overall job measured	No point values	Classification	Straight and paired-comparison ranking
	Point values assigned	—	—
Elements or factors of the job measured	No point values	—	Factor-guided ranking
	Point values assigned	Point plans	Factor comparison

The Ranking System

One widely used method of job evaluation is the system which simply ranks one job against another without assigning point values. The evaluator compares two jobs, one with the other, and judges which is the more difficult. Once this determination has been made, another job is compared with the first two and a similar decision is made. The process is repeated until all jobs have been ranked, from the most difficult down to the least.

The simplicity of the ranking system is its greatest asset. Little preparation is required, and the evaluation process is rapid and inexpensive. The ranking system also utilizes job-against-job comparison. This is the most accurate method of evaluation because it is far easier to judge which of two jobs is the more difficult than it is to judge the absolute difficulty of either.

Unfortunately, the very simplicity of the ranking method is also its greatest weakness. The system does little to guide the judgment of evaluators; there is a tendency to judge each job on the basis of its dominant characteristic or factor, so that inconsistencies can multiply. In addition, the results are extremely difficult to explain or justify either to employees or to managers because there is no record of the judgments of the evaluators. Finally, the ranking system can only indicate that one job is more difficult than another, without specifying in any way how much more difficult it is.

In order to refine the ranking system to some extent, several techniques have been evolved. One of these is paired-comparison ranking, in which each evaluator is given a list that pairs every job with every other job and is asked to select which job in each pair ranks higher. In Exhibition 5, for example, the selection is bookkeeper over clerk-typist A, secretary over clerk-typist A, and so on. The results are analyzed statistically to produce a master list of rankings.

EXHIBIT 5
PAIRED-COMPARISON RANKINGS

[*Italics indicate the higher-ranking in each pair of jobs*]

Bookkeeper	Clerk-typist A
Clerk-typist A	*Secretary*
Telephone operator	Mail clerk
Clerk-typist A	*Telephone operator*
Telephone operator	*Secretary*
Telephone operator	*Bookkeeper*
Secretary	Mail clerk
Bookkeeper	*Secretary*
Mail clerk	*Bookkeeper*
Mail clerk	*Clerk-typist A*

Another refinement of straight ranking is the factor-guided ranking technique. Under this system, the evaluators again rank job against job but in terms of predetermined factors. In other words, instead of ranking jobs solely by overall difficulty, they rank separately for different elements of difficulty which are called "factors" —such as knowledge and physical effort required. When the evaluation is completed, there is a separate ranking for each factor which was identified, and these rankings can be used as an audit to check the overall rankings.

The Classification System

In the classification system (sometimes called the rating system), the job is measured against a predetermined yardstick whose various divisions define overall job values or difficulty. The evaluators compare each job with the yardstick and slot the job into the grade which best describes its characteristics and difficulty. While this system is simple and inexpensive to install and administer, it is used very seldom. For one thing, it has most of the shortcomings of the ranking system. For another, it is fantastically difficult to define levels of overall job worth in any meaningful way.

The classification system was one of the first to be developed and was useful when a relatively large number of employees worked at relatively few jobs. As the number and diversity of jobs increased, the system became less effective because of the increasing difficulty of defining the yardstick. On the other hand, as described in Chapter VIII, it has recently had some use in evaluating professional jobs.

The Point-Evaluation System

The point-evaluation system is probably the most widely used in business today. Under this system, various factors of a group of jobs are selected and defined. A separate yardstick describing different degrees of each is prepared, and a job is then ranked against every yardstick. In essence, this is the same process as the classification system except that the job is evaluated on a separate scale for each factor and point weightings are assigned.

The type of factor yardstick used in point plans is illustrated in Exhibit 6. In evaluating jobs, the analyst simply studies the job duties and compares them with the yardstick. He then assigns the job the degree which seems to describe best the extent to which the factor is important. This process is repeated for each factor, and the point values of each factor degree are totaled.

The point system has a number of advantages over the

EXHIBIT 6
YARDSTICK IN A POINT-EVALUATION PLAN

Factor: Know-how
Considerations: Educational background and amount of experience necessary for satisfactory performance on a given job

Degree	Description	Points
1	Requires only average learning ability and good aptitude for factory operations; an average of three weeks' learning period needed for satisfactory performance; ability to follow instructions and perform repetitive operations under periodic check is essential.	28
2	Instructions more varied but still of a routine nature; typical of job with a more diverse work cycle or where minor adjustments to equipment are involved; a basic general shop knowledge gained through previous experience in such jobs as machine operation, methodized assembly, or inspection work required.	56
3	Some specific knowledge, such as blueprint reading and use of adjustable gauges, required; an aptitude for understanding machine operations and shop problems is necessary; calls for systematic training on the job.	84
4	Requires some technical knowledge as gained through formal trade school courses and previous shop experience; some advanced technical school training in mathematics and machine shop techniques required; a thorough knowledge of plant operations, equipment, and extensive on-the-job training in a variety of phases of shop work are necessary.	112
5	Requires extensive technical knowledge gained through formal training and/or related instruction in advanced technical information (including a complete high school education plus a full apprenticeship training); requires ability to perform diverse tasks subject to only occasional check.	140

less refined ranking and classification systems. The use of fixed, predetermined, and defined factors forces the evaluator to consider the same job elements when rating every job. Furthermore, the assignment of point values indicates not only which job is worth more than another, but how much more it is worth. Finally, a record of the judgments of the evaluator is available later for explaining the results of the evaluation to supervisors and employees alike.

Just how useful a point-evaluation system is in guiding the judgment of the evaluator depends upon the factors which are selected for use and the accuracy of the point values assigned. In addition, there is the problem of establishing the correct number of degrees: ideally, there should be just enough to identify minimum measurable differences in the factor. Another special problem of point plans is that of defining each of these degrees clearly so that they will serve as a meaningful guide to evaluators and also provide an understandable explanation of the slottings which have been made.

The Factor-Comparison System

A fourth basic system which has been widely used in business is factor comparison, in which the various factors are compared simply on a job-by-job basis, without definitions for the various degrees. In other words, the evaluators analyze and rank all jobs in terms of one factor, then rank all in relation to a second factor, and so forth until rankings have been established for each of the factors used. Since point values have already been given to various degrees of rankings, it is necessary only to total the points assigned to a job under each of the factors in order to get the job's overall relative worth.

Factor comparison has two basic advantages. First, it

uses the job-by-job comparison technique. Second, it does not involve the problems of semantics encountered in building factor yardsticks, since the various degrees do not have to be defined. However, because of this lack of definitions, the results of evaluation under the factor-comparison system are more difficult to explain to employees or to supervisors who question the classifications.

Combination and Special Systems

Many companies have combined features of the point-evaluation and factor-comparison methods to gain the advantages of both. Even where this is not done formally, as in accordance with company policy, it is frequently done by individual evaluators or managers in order to insure the best results. In effect, the combination system usually involves slotting all jobs by means of a point plan and then auditing these results through a job-by-job comparison within each factor. While the process entails a double evaluation, the results usually justify the extra effort.

Some companies use multiple evaluation plans as a required part of wage and salary administration. One such program calls for evaluation of each position three times by three different factor-comparison plans. If the results in each case are not identical, the evaluations are reviewed and adjusted. This involves triple work, and the incremental increase in precision must be weighed against the cost.

The market evaluation system identifies bench-mark company jobs comparable with jobs in available pay surveys. The percent relationship of pay in the market becomes the percent relationship of total points in evaluation. Bench-mark jobs are then evaluated by one of the traditional methods just described, but results must conform to the market. These bench-mark job evaluations then become the yardstick against which all other jobs are evaluated. The unique advantage of the system is that the market is built into the program from the start, thereby insuring that evaluation results will conform to the realities of the marketplace. Evaluators must make sure, however, that the survey data are valid and that bench-mark jobs do not reflect unusual or temporary market conditions.

USE OF JOB EVALUATION

Job evaluation is the cornerstone of a formal wage and salary program. Without realistically determining relative job worth in some specific and reasonably defensible manner, it would be most difficult, if not impossible, to establish a formal program. Specifically, the job evaluation process plays a key role in wage and salary administration in the following ways:

1. It is the most effective means of determining internal pay relationships.
2. It can be used as an instrument for effecting the company's basic pay policies.
3. Equitable base-pay relationships set by job evaluation serve as a foundation for incentive or bonus plans or merit increase programs.
4. Job evaluation provides a reasonable basis for personnel moves. Unless relative job levels are correct, managers will not really know whether a personnel move represents a promotion, a transfer, or a demotion.
5. Useful controls over wage and salary costs can be greatly aided by job evaluation.
6. Job evaluation provides a realistic foundation for gearing company pay scales to the wages paid by competing companies.

7. Job evaluation assists managers in meeting day-to-day pay problems. This in turn contributes to the reduction of employee grievances, to higher employee productivity through higher morale, and to decreased turnover.
8. By providing a framework for decision making and a method of control, job evaluation makes it possible to delegate more pay decisions, and thus conserves the time of top management.

These are the substantial advantages to be gained from job evaluation. However, the establishment of a job evaluation program may mean a substantial increase in costs —the salaries of the wage and salary staff personnel, the time that managers devote to the evaluation process, the administrative costs inherent in a formal evaluation program, and costs for outside consulting services which may be needed. Top management must, of course, weigh these costs against the potential benefits.

Problems of Design

Although most of the technical problems associated with designing a job evaluation plan are primarily the concern of the staff specialist and consultant, two have great significance in terms of overall objectives. These are: (1) selection of the factors which are to be used to measure job difficulty and (2) the assignment of point values.

As for the selection of factors, experience has shown that there are a number of requirements:
- Each factor must have some relationship to job difficulty or job value.
- In combination, they should correlate reasonably well with job difficulty.
- The factors selected must be both observable and measurable.

- Important elements of every job must be measured by one or more factors.
- Every factor should serve to help distinguish between jobs.
- Two factors should not measure essentially the same characteristic.

The assignment of point values within each factor is also important, because in effect they establish the relative significance of the factors used in the plan. For example, if the maximum assigned to the factor "know-how" is 200 points, and the maximum assigned to "working conditions" is 100 points, then the plan says, in effect, that know-how can be twice as important as working conditions in determining the difficulty of the jobs measured.

There is no one correct set of factors or point weightings. Many different combinations have been used successfully. Ideally, factors and weightings should be geared to the level and nature of jobs covered, the type of business, and similar considerations. Therefore, it is dangerous to copy an existing plan, even if it is has been successful elsewhere, unless pertinent conditions are similar.

It is apparent, even from this brief description of the two major technical problems, that the job evaluation yardstick is essentially a matter of human judgment. The yardstick itself, as well as the job evaluation process, is basically subjective: Unless the difficult decisions involved are made by experienced persons, the plan can result in distorted pay relationships or can become an administrative burden without purpose.

Problems of Use

There are a number of common problems of measurement which may be encountered by evaluators. For instance, most jobs include heterogeneous duties which are difficult for the evaluator to measure. If these duties were evaluated separately, they would frequently result in different job classifications. As a general rule in such cases, evaluation is based upon the principal duty performed as a regular part of the assigned job. In this way—assuming, as should be so, that the job incumbent spends most of his time working at his highest level of skill—credit is given for the highest skill the job requires.

A similar problem, frequently encountered in smaller organizations, is the "combination job" in which two or more completely separate sets of duties are performed by one individual. In hourly-paid jobs each set is often evaluated separately, and employees are paid at different rates according to the number of hours spent at the different types of work. For most salaried jobs, however, this is not practical; actually, the job is classified and evaluated on the basis of the higher-level or more difficult position.

A third problem is whether or not jobs should be measured on the basis of minimum, average, or maximum requirements. Generally speaking, the evaluation is based upon minimum job requirements because of the great difficulty of determining either average or maximum requirements. So long as all jobs are measured consistently in terms of minimum requirements, the final results of evaluation will not be influenced.

Evaluators face situations in which some jobs are really not judged by the rules. Frequently, for instance, secretarial positions are classified strictly on the basis of the boss's stature, regardless of the work actually assigned. As a result, a secretary to a vice president may be classified as an executive secretary even though she never takes shorthand and really is assigned only low-level clerical work. Other occupations also present unique problems of evaluation. For example, technicians are frequently classified in a manner inconsistent with the job evaluation program, owing to the fact that the duties are not rigidly defined. Such employees may be moved from one assignment to another on the basis of their personal background, the quality of the work they are capable of performing, and the work which is available. The problem of classifying people in these categories is somewhat similar to the problem, discussed in Chapter VIII, of evaluating engineering and other professional jobs.

Finally, there are a number of special evaluation problems which a company may face. In rapidly growing organizational units, for instance, it may not be possible to specify the exact job duties, and the work assigned may depend to some extent upon the types of persons who can be recruited. Again, changes in organization or technological methods may cause mass upgradings or downgradings. What may be good evaluation technique in these circumstances may be very bad business practice. Finally, trainee positions may exist where a straightforward evaluation of the job duties assigned would result in unrealistic classifications, considering the types of persons selected for such assignments.

Accuracy of Results

Unfortunately, there is no objective method of discovering just how precise job evaluation is in determining relative job worth. It is not possible to *measure* the accuracy of job evaluation; it is possible only to *judge* accuracy. There are a number of practical tests that the manager may apply in judging the accuracy of his own job evaluation program:
1. Does it result in pay relationships more logical than those which might exist without it?
2. Does it facilitate the solution of daily problems?

3. Are results acceptable to employees?
4. Does job evaluation contribute to that rather indefinable quality of good human relations?
5. Does it help to answer or to avoid employee grievances concerning pay classifications?
6. Do the results of evaluation agree reasonably with established paths of job progression?
7. Do results correspond realistically with existing market pay relationships?
8. Does the evaluation program tie in with the company's operating needs?
9. Do the results justify the additional costs?
10. Does evaluation provide top management with a technique which helps put company policies into effect? At the same time, does it provide reasonable control of company wage costs?

The final test of accuracy is that of management experience. Does job evaluation guide managers to make reasonable judgments with respect to relative job worth? Observation of many programs and their results, particularly in the past few years, leads to the conclusion that with a sound evaluation plan two reasonable men, both of whom know the job being measured, will not disagree on more than one of ten factor judgments. This means that there will probably not be differences of more than one pay level in more than one job in 30. In any judgmental exercise, this represents a high degree of "accuracy."

Improving Results

The usefulness and accuracy of the job evaluation program depend upon how well the program is conceived, how well it is geared to the individual company's situation, and how well the evaluations are carried out. This last, in effect, is a question of how well managers use the evaluation tools which have been provided. There are various techniques which are useful in increasing the accuracy and usefulness of evaluation results.

The very order in which jobs are evaluated frequently helps to improve the quality of evaluation. The first should be those with which evaluators are generally familiar and in which the duties are fairly standard. The evaluation of these easier jobs can then be used as an additional yardstick for slotting other jobs. After the better-understood jobs have been evaluated, it is helpful to select "families" of jobs, which might include, for instance, all bookkeeping and accounting positions. It is usually easier and more accurate to compare jobs in the same family because the duties are somewhat related.

Evaluators have also found that it helps to employ not only multiple evaluation but cross-evaluation as well. Multiple evaluation merely means evaluating jobs two different times by the same technique. The results of the two evaluations are then compared, and the differences are resolved. Cross-evaluation also involves evaluating the same groups of jobs more than once but with two different techniques.

Line managers and staff specialists can use this cross-evaluation in various ways. For instance, if the jobs were originally evaluated by the point system, they could be cross-evaluated by:
- Ranking all jobs by total point values assigned and inspecting the results of this ranking.
- Grouping all jobs whose total point values fall within a relatively narrow point range and checking each grouping to see if an overall judgment indicates that they are worth about the same pay.

- Comparing the factor-by-factor slotting of a few jobs, in the same general family but in different departments, to see if differences can really be justified.
- Examining all jobs which have been assigned the same degree of the same factor to see if the slotting is valid.

In order to increase the effectiveness of evaluation, it is important to avoid some common errors. In one of the most frequent, the evaluator forms preconceived notions about where a job should fit and then proceeds to justify them. This is a little like cheating at solitaire, and those who are guilty of this error might ask themselves what plan was used to arrive at the preconceived notions. Care must also be taken to evaluate the job rather than the individual on the job. Finally, it is important to avoid the "halo effect," that is, the tendency of an evaluator to be influenced in all his ranking of a job by the rank which he assigned to the job's dominant factor.

Each of these techniques helps the evaluator to increase the effectiveness of his evaluations. However, all of them are dependent upon his know-how and his conscientiousness. Perfunctory or hurried evaluations do not yield satisfactory results; evaluators must have the time to do the job and must be required to do it well.

Finally, any system can be useful only if it is used. Every manager should use the plan, and management must agree to require that it be used. If someone has a better system, let him propose it; then his may become the system used by everyone.

The Manager's Role

Managers always participate in the job evaluation process to some extent. Just how they participate, and how much, will depend upon circumstances. Most companies have assigned the responsibility for evaluation decisions to staff specialists because of these significant advantages: Specialization generally means greater efficiency; staff specialists tend to be more objective; greater consistency is obtained when a limited number of persons interpret and apply the job evaluation plan in different departments; and staff specialists are held strictly accountable for results.

Even when staff specialists evaluate jobs, line managers still have the basic responsibility for reviewing both the job analysis and the results of job evaluation. This review carries with it the authority to approve or appeal. (It is interesting to note, however, that a few companies have recently had good results from reversing the traditional line/staff roles in job evaluation. Under this plan, line supervisors have the responsibility to make evaluation decisions, and staff has the right to review and appeal.)

Managers also have the obligation of keeping the program up to date. It is vital that they report changes in organization, job assignments, and methods of work to insure that classifications are kept current.

In carrying out the program, managers should not try to circumvent the system in order to obtain what may seem like operating advantages. For instance, the manager who presses for identical classifications for large numbers of his jobs may think that this will ease the problem of assigning employees to jobs and avoid employee complaints. Actually, he is creating inequities in pay relationships which will probably result in problems far greater than any small advantages from leveling. Another tempting, but highly dangerous, practice is to seek the solution of basic personnel problems by artificially upgrading employees. The manager who yields to employees' pleas or threats or to the pressure of circumstances, and who attempts to solve difficult personnel problems in this manner, is only creating inequities which will inevitably give more trouble in the future.

Individual managers have a fundamental responsibility for explaining job evaluation to employees. It is neither possible nor necessary for the manager to make job evaluation experts out of employees; but he should see that they understand such basic aspects of job evaluation as these:

- The reasons why the company established a job evaluation program.
- The way job evaluation works.
- The fact that it is concerned with measuring the job, not the person on the job.
- The fact that it seeks only to establish relative job worth.
- The fact that the job evaluation plan is applied consistently to all jobs.
- The factors which are used to determine relative job worth and how and why they were selected.

Staff personnel can help explain job evaluation by preparing booklets or by holding employee meetings. It is the supervisor, however, who is the closest to his employees, and he should know best what they do not understand about the plan. Furthermore, he can take advantage of individual questions or grievances to re-explain and resell the program.

QUESTIONS AND ANSWERS

How well the supervisor handles day-to-day questions can have a major effect on the success of the plan. While innumerable types of questions arise in relation to specific evaluation programs, there are certain basic ones which

JOB EVALUATION

are likely to be asked again and again. Some of these are outlined in the following section, together with suggested ways of answering them.

QUESTION 1: Why is my job [purchasing clerk] only in level 8?

Suggestions for answering:
a. Make sure that the employee is not rationalizing some other question or complaint. Try to find out why this question was raised. In other words, make sure you know what the question is before you answer it.
b. Review the job description with employee. Make sure that you and he agree on what job duties are assigned.
c. If possible, go through the evaluation step by step. Where point plans are used, let the employee read the degree definition of the category in which his job was slotted, and explain to him why the job was slotted in this way.

QUESTION 2: Why aren't the bookkeepers paid as much as the stenographers?

Suggestions for answering:
a. Try first to handle like Question 1; that is, try to convince the employee that his job is correctly evaluated.
b. If necessary, show the employee his job description and the description of the job or jobs which he is comparing with his own.
c. Make a comparison of each factor and explain the reasons why the other job was rated higher.
d. It is not always necessary to get an employee to agree with the relative rating or slotting of each factor. He must, however, understand that the evaluator made the necessary comparisons on a systematic basis and that he did have good reasons for distinguishing between the jobs.
e. Managers should also keep in mind that this type of complaint may arise because of the inferior performance of another employee or because of some personal conflict between employees.

QUESTION 3: Why is it that the job analyst set the rate for my job without ever seeing it?

> *Suggestions for answering:*
> a. The first thing the supervisor should do, of course, is to make sure that the evaluator did actually observe the job to some extent or received information from someone who did have firsthand knowledge.
> b. The supervisor should sit down with the employee and go over the job description with him to satisfy him that the description is really accurate.
> c. The supervisor may have to point out to him that it is only necessary to observe the work performed by one employee in order to determine the job duties of all employees doing the same work.

QUESTION 4: Don't you think that an inspector should get a higher rate of pay than a material handler, because the inspector job requires visual attention and greater know-how?

> *Suggestions for answering:*
> a. The supervisor should, of course, point out that all jobs must be evaluated by a consistent set of factors—that it is just as incorrect to evaluate all jobs on the basis of physical effort (for the benefit of material handlers) as it would be to evaluate all jobs on the basis of those factors which are important in the inspector's job.
> b. It might also be valuable either to review the evaluation of the inspector's job or to make a factor-by-factor comparison between the inspector's job and the material handler's job.

QUESTION 5: What determines job levels?

> *Suggestion for answering:*
> The task here is to give the employee the basic information about job evaluation which has been outlined earlier.

JOB EVALUATION

QUESTION 6: What is my pay grade?

Suggestion for answering:

It is unfortunate that in some companies an unnecessary secrecy surrounds the job evaluation program. We can never gain employee understanding and acceptance of the program where this is true. Those who think they will avoid trouble by not explaining the plan are merely insuring that it will never succeed. The only real solution is to tell the employee what the grade is.

QUESTION 7: The girls in the billing department are in the same pay grade as we sales clerks, yet we work much harder.

Suggestions for answering:
a. Point out that employees and managers alike sometimes find it difficult to separate man worth from job worth in their thinking.
b. The supervisor must explain that job evaluation seeks to establish relative job worth and has nothing to do with the effort or energy expended by the individual employee on that job.
c. It is hoped that the supervisor will be able to outline the merit rating or incentive program by which the company rewards employees for individual contributions.
d. Finally, it is usually wise to review the classification of the job involved and perhaps even make a factor-by-factor comparison of the sales clerk's and billing clerk's jobs.

QUESTION 8: Since my job was evaluated, you have assigned me additional work. Shouldn't my job be upgraded?

Suggestions for answering:
a. An additional duty does not necessarily change the evaluation or classification, but it almost always raises the question in the mind of the employee.

b. First, make certain the additional duty was incorporated in the description, provided that it is an assigned and permanent item.
   c. Make sure the change was or is evaluated.
   d. Then handle as in Question 1.

QUESTION 9: You have me do a greater variety of things than Smith, yet we are in the same pay grade.

   Suggestions for answering:
   a. Review description and evaluation as above.
   b. Make the point that variety does not necessarily mean more value.

QUESTION 10: I fill in for the boss when he is out; shouldn't I be in a higher grade?

   Suggestion for answering:

   To the extent that employees are given assignments to broaden their experience or train them for bigger jobs, this represents an investment and should not be reflected in higher pay grades. Those who "fill in" for the boss seldom handle all his responsibilities. But, if the duty is a regular one, concerns more than a few weeks of the year, and involves higher responsibilities, it should be reflected in the description and the evaluation.

By effectively answering such questions as these, the supervisor is able to gain employee acceptance of the program. Without such acceptance, it is difficult to see how the job evaluation program can make any of the contributions to company operations that are generally sought.

CHAPTER III

THE SECOND STEP: PRICING JOB VALUE

AFTER JOB EVALUATION HAS ESTABLISHED THE RELATIVE difficulty of jobs within the company in terms of points or rankings, the next step is to translate these into a pay structure. This step involves three processes: fixing pay grades, pricing them, and setting up pay ranges.

The Techniques and Their Purposes

The procedure for establishing pay grades is illustrated in Exhibit 7. The results of evaluation (column A) are merely a list of jobs from the highest-rated, which received 427 points in the evaluation plan, down to the lowest-rated, which received only 170 points. Theoretically, it is possible to give dollar values to these jobs in some direct proportion to the points assigned. This is administratively impractical, however, because there would be almost as many different pay grades as there were jobs in the company. Also, since even very small changes in duties would

WAGES AND SALARIES

EXHIBIT 7:

	Step 1: Column A	Step 2: Column B	Step 3: Column C
	Evaluation Results:	*Group Jobs:*	*Grade Jobs:*
STEP IN PRICING PROCESS	Express pay relationships only in terms of total point values for each job evaluated.	Choose logical cutoff points; group jobs with about the same number of point values. Determine cutoff points by number of grades needed, job groupings, labor-market pay relationships.	Establish pay grade by "best fit" point groupings. Develop smooth progression (40 points per pay grade) for consistent and impartial treatment.
ILLUSTRATION OF STEP IN PRICING OF PAY STRUCTURE	Job A 427 points Job B 427 points Job C 418 points	418–427 points	Grade 7: 401 or more points
	Job D 382 points Job E 379 points Job F 362 points	362–382 points	Grade 6: 361–400 points
	Job G 359 points Job H 340 points Job I 338 points	338–359 points	Grade 5: 321–360 points
	Job J 299 points Job K 297 points Job L 295 points Job M 291 points Job N 291 points Job O 283 points	283–299 points	Grade 4: 281–320 points
	Job P 250 points	250 points	Grade 3: 241–280 points
	Job Q 223 points	223 points	Grade 2: 201–240 points
	Job R 190 points Job S 188 points Job T 170 points	170–190 points	Grade 1: Under 200 points

PRICING JOB VALUE

Pricing the Pay Structure

	Step 4: Column D *Conduct Survey:* Select "key jobs" and survey comparable companies.	Step 5: Column E *Establish Base Rates:* Determine "best fit" from wage survey consistent with basic company wage policy.	Step 6: Column F *Establish Pay Ranges:* Provide for individual compensation on the basis of merit or length of service (15% spread; 6% between grades).
Key Job Used	Results of Survey (Average Hourly Rate Paid)		
A	$2.53	$2.49	$2.34–$2.70
E	$2.48	$2.34	$2.21–$2.54
H	$2.21	$2.22	$2.08–$2.40
K	$2.09	—	—
M	$2.16	$2.10	$1.97–$2.27
P	$1.91	$1.98	$1.85–$2.13
Q	—	$1.86	$1.75–$2.02
S	$1.68	$1.74	$1.65–$1.90

probably require adjustments in pay, pay grades would be changing constantly. In any event, the results of job evaluation can never be accurate enough to justify such fine distinctions, so that for technical as well as administrative reasons, jobs should be grouped in pay grades.

The actual establishment of these pay grades is a complex process. Fundamentally, it involves grouping in such a way as to: place jobs of the same general value in the same grade; insure that jobs of distinctly different value are in different grades; provide for a smooth progression of point groupings; fit realistically into the existing apportionment of pay within the company; and conform reasonably to pay patterns in the labor market area.

This means, technically speaking, that the results of job evaluation are first inspected to locate the natural cutoff points (column B of Exhibit 7) and to be sure the groupings are reasonable and logical. The smooth progression that is the best fit statistically is then determined (column C), and these results are again inspected for logical internal relationships. They are also checked against the actual relationships existing in the labor market. In other words, it is necessary to inspect both the results of job evaluation and the labor market survey before determining final cutoff points.

After this process is completed, all jobs that fall within the cutoff points defining a pay grade will be considered to have the same basic value. For instance, in Exhibit 7 all jobs which total between 361 and 400 evaluation points are placed in pay grade 6. While administratively sound, this process raises some difficulties. It is relatively easy to defend the placing of job D (382 points) and job E (379 points) in the same pay grade. The difficulty comes in explaining why job F (362 points) is in grade 6, but job G (359 points) is only in grade 5. Actually such distinctions can be justified only on a practical basis—if pay grades are to be established at all, there must be some cutoff points. Borderline jobs will always exist, and as long as point groupings are based on a smooth progression, the cutoff points are at least consistent and impartial. Borderline cases should be reviewed most carefully, however. Many companies follow the course of giving the job the next higher ranking whenever a borderline case creates a reasonable doubt.

Once jobs have been grouped into pay grades, it is possible to price them all by surveying key jobs. Not every position can be surveyed, because many of the jobs in a company are unique. When jobs have been grouped, however, only a limited number need to be priced in order to set up the entire pay structure. In Exhibit 7, seven of the jobs in column D are assumed to be comparable to jobs found in the other companies which will be surveyed. Since jobs D, E, and F have been grouped into grade 6, we know that they are all to receive the same pay, which is set when job E is priced.

From the survey of other companies, base rates for each pay grade are established. In Exhibit 7, the actual rates (column E) represent the "best fit" in the survey results. It was assumed that the company wanted to establish a pay structure equal to the average rates paid by the companies surveyed. The rates in column E reflect this policy and result in a smooth percent progression in base pay between grades.

Pay ranges can then be established around these base rates. In Exhibit 7, for example, the rates were used as the midpoint for the ranges. With pay ranges, individual compensation based on performance and other considerations becomes possible. Ranges also give the company needed flexibility.

Pricing the Structure: The Wage Survey

The pricing of pay grades involves questions of both basic company policy and survey techniques. There are various factors relating to company operations and objectives which must be considered—financial characteristics, growth objectives, profitability, and the nature of the firm's operations. Some students of wage and salary administration believe that these considerations should be the primary determinants of pay policy. The traditional emphasis, however, is on competitive pay. Certainly, the company must take into account pay for similar work in other companies, not only for reasons of equity but also to make sure that pay levels are sufficient to attract and retain qualified people. The primary method of doing this is through the use of pay surveys.

Surveys take many forms and vary considerably, depending upon their purpose. For any type of pay survey, however, it is necessary, first, to determine the companies to be surveyed; second, to select the jobs to be surveyed; third, to decide what supplemental data should be obtained; and, finally, to conduct the survey in a technically sound fashion.

Which companies are chosen can be the genuinely critical factor, for if they lack significance in terms of the purpose of the survey, the results will be meaningless. Actually, in a large number of labor markets almost any conclusion can be proved by carefully selecting the companies to be examined. For valid results, firms should be chosen on the basis of such questions as these:

- Does the company really compete for available talent? Have any of your own employees left to go to it—or vice versa?

PRICING JOB VALUE

- Are the company's operations comparable with yours? Are there enough jobs in common to make the survey reasonable?
- Is the company a product-market competitor?
- Is the company large enough to provide a sufficient number of comparisons to make the survey meaningful?
- Does the company have a reasonably sound wage and salary program? If not, the results may be a meaningless hodgepodge of rates.
- Can the company be counted on to cooperate by supplying accurate and reliable data?

Under the best of conditions, selecting companies for survey is not an easy task. To complicate matters, most businesses operate not in one labor market but in a number of different markets. For example, even among management personnel, the market for manufacturing managers may be very different from the market for financial managers.

After the problem of choosing suitable companies has been met, the next task is to select similar jobs for comparison. The usual technique is to pick out key jobs within the company which is conducting the survey and to get rates for comparable jobs in each of the companies being studied. "Key jobs" in this case means jobs which represent a good cross section of the pay structure. Ideally, there should be at least one job from each pay classification. Key jobs should also represent those which are usually found in the companies to be surveyed. Finally, it is useful if they constitute a sampling of jobs in the various operating units of the company.

The value of the survey data depends to a considerable extent on how carefully these jobs are selected and how well the key jobs match jobs in the cooperating companies. In order to make sure that there is a good matching, it is generally necessary to write out clear job descriptions and to visit the companies surveyed in order to make detailed comparisons of the jobs and their rates of pay.

After the great volume of data has been collected, it is the unhappy task of an analyst first to tabulate and then to present the information. In cases where it is to be presented to management, he usually prepares a summary which points up major findings and conclusions.

A typical format for such a summary is shown in Exhibit 8 (based on data shown in Exhibit 7), where the data collected are compared with the recommended company pay structure. Charts like this one provide management with a clear picture of how its rates compare with other rates paid in the area surveyed. Such data can, of course, be quite misleading unless management has some understanding of the method of collection and the statistical composition of the material. The information in Exhibit 8 does not, for instance, give the *total* market-area picture; it represents only the rates paid by those companies surveyed. This may be a small proportion of the total in large market areas. Furthermore, only the quartile range is shown, not the total dispersion of rates. Conceivably these quartile range figures, while they represent 50 percent of the jobs, may represent only 10 percent of the dispersion of rates paid by the companies surveyed. Finally, the data as shown give no indication of how many rates were reported, whether there was good coverage in each pay grade, whether all companies surveyed gave information relating to each grade, or whether a few large companies dominated any of the data presented. Presumably, the staff specialists obtained the best information available, but it could contain statistical imperfections and should merely be regarded as indicative of the labor market pay situation.

EXHIBIT 8

Data from Area Wage Survey Compared with Recommended Company Pay Structure

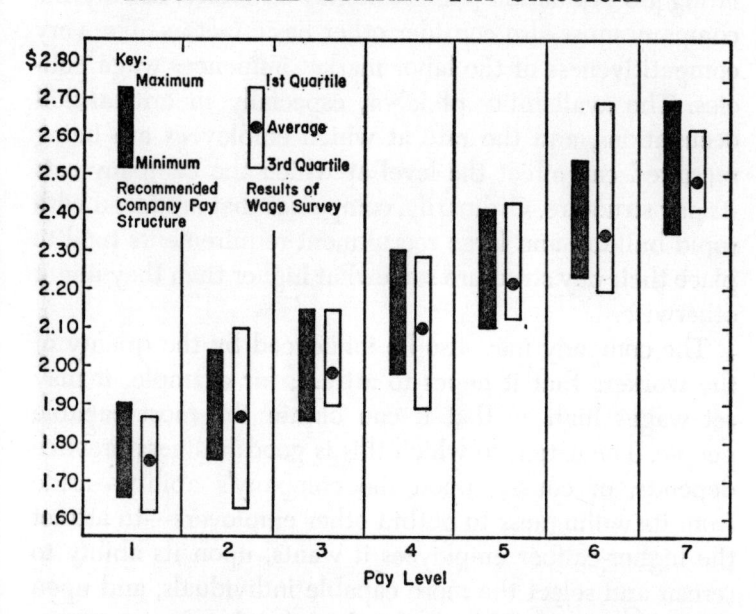

Recent studies, for instance, indicate that survey findings are accurate within 5 percent for clerical positions and 10 percent for top-level positions when the best survey techniques are utilized. The same studies show typical dispersion from highest pay to lowest pay (even excluding the top and bottom 10 percent) to be over 50 percent for clerical positions and as much as 200 percent for management positions. Thus even the best surveys are not scientifically accurate, and management has considerable latitude in setting a "competitive pay structure."

Pricing the Structure: Other Considerations

While the wage survey is an important factor in translating job evaluation points into pay structure, usually the company must also consider other basic factors. The very competitiveness of the labor market influences wage policies. The availability of labor, especially in critical-skill occupations, and the rate at which employees are being recruited can affect the level at which the company sets its pay structure. Ordinarily, companies that are faced with rapid buildup and large recruitment requirements tend to place their pay structure somewhat higher than they might otherwise.

The company may also be influenced by the quality of the workers that it hopes to attract; for example, it may set wages high so that it can obtain the most capable people. The extent to which this is good business practice depends, of course, upon the company's ability—aside from its willingness to outbid other employers—to attract the higher-caliber employees it wants, upon its ability to screen and select the more capable individuals, and upon its ability to utilize them. On the other hand, a company may deliberately choose to go into the labor market area with wages which are geared only to the average, on the assumption that average proficiency will serve the company's needs. Management may even intentionally pay wages which are somewhat below the average because it believes that it can still attract the number of workers that it needs, or because of the economics and competitiveness of its own business as compared with others in the labor market area.

Companies attempt to keep their structure somewhat competitive with product competitors. Here again, however, a company does have some choice, because high wages do not necessarily mean high wage costs. The importance of product-competitor factors depends mainly on the competitive nature of the business, but it should also be influenced by such considerations as the following: productivity levels, the ratio of wage costs to total costs, the present level of profits, business forecasts, the ability to pass on higher wage costs to customers through price increases, and product differentiation.

There are other operations-oriented considerations which may be relevant under certain conditions. Companies may, for instance, use pay administration to encourage employees to move into certain types of work or areas of the business. Such company strategy can affect policies of pay level as well as pay form.

Changes in wages over a period of time must also be taken into account. If a company tends to increase its wages at a faster or slower rate than others, this can, of course, help or hinder its future efforts in recruiting, and can affect business competition. Finally, a company must consider pay changes because employees are sensitive to them. General wage increases have gained considerable publicity, particularly in recent years. When employees read or hear about increases which are more generous than those made by their own company, their morale suffers, and the turnover rate may increase as well. General across-the-board increases, where all employees receive the same increase on either a cents-per-hour or percentage basis, are widespread, especially in jobs where employees are paid a flat rate, where pay is low, and where promotional opportunities are limited. Many unions, of course, prefer general increases, both as a means of demonstrating their own usefulness to members and as a substitute for discretionary decisions by management.

Employees are extremely conscious of changes in the

cost of living. They recognize that unless wages increase at least as fast as the cost of living increases, their standard of living will decline. In a dynamic economy such as ours, people are accustomed to expect a continued increase in their standard of living. They therefore tend to look to the company for wage increases which outpace increases in living costs.

It should be apparent even from this brief summary that a company cannot depend solely upon the results of a labor market wage survey to carry out its wage policy. All of the considerations which have been mentioned are important in company pay decisions and should be given some weight when the pay structure is established or changed.

Characteristics of Traditional Structures

A company's pay structure ordinarily looks something like the one in Exhibit 8. Since managers must use this structure to make pay decisions, it is essential that they acquire some knowledge of its basic characteristics.

Several technical features deserve attention. The minimum in each level, of course, should roughly reflect the pay needed to hire most persons with minimum qualifications in that grade. The progression from the minimum of one grade to the minimum of the next highest will vary depending on the job, the labor market, and the job grading. The usual variations are from 5 to 7 percent for hourly jobs, 7 to 10 percent for office jobs, and 8 to 12 percent for exempt positions. Of equal importance, particularly to the operating manager, is the fact that this progression should represent the same percentage spread between all labor grades, or some equally logical system.

Otherwise, it will be impossible for managers to explain or justify pay ranges.

The within-grade spread will vary depending upon two factors: the company's method of compensating individual performance on the job and the opportunity an employee has to make an extra contribution. When the company does have an employee merit-pay policy, the range will tend to be greater for higher-level jobs. The logic here is that higher-level managers, for instance, have a greater opportunity than mail clerks to exercise initiative, efficient work habits, and other qualities which increase personal productivity.* As a result, the within-grade spread for hourly jobs will vary from 10 to 25 percent for office positions from 25 to 35 percent and for management positions from 30 to as much as 100 percent. This means that there is generally an overlap of three to four pay grades in most situations; that is, the maximum of a pay grade will be within the range of a grade which is three or four levels higher.

The maximums in these within-grade ranges are particularly difficult to establish; they are even more difficult to defend. There is some theoretical maximum for every job, and regardless of how well a person performs the work, he will reach a point at which further improvement either is limited by the very nature of the duties assigned or adds nothing to the operation. The reasoning—except, perhaps, in higher-level management positions—is really irrefutable. The questions are always: At what point should these maximums be established? How should they be administered? What does the manager do with person who gets to the top of his range?

* Some also argue that pay ranges should be greater in higher-level jobs because the opportunity for promotion is less, but there are very few cases in which this view is sound and reasonable.

There is no scientific means of determining where maximums should be placed. As indicated, the pay ranges should reflect to some extent the individual's potential contribution on the job. The company can also be guided by the maximums reported by other companies in the area. Regardless of what maximums are set, however, managers still face the problems of the employee at the top of his pay grade. For a person with potential for greater responsibility, the ideal solution is to promote him. Because higher positions are not always available at a given time, managers should start exploring the possibilities for promotion before such an employee reaches the maximum of his range. Frequently the manager must take a broader company view and be willing to part with a capable person who deserves promotion.

Actually, promotional opportunities are almost always available for high-talent employees in a fair-size company, unless business is declining. Few growing companies have such an overabundance of able workers that the manager cannot, with some planning, take advantage of their talents. Promotions need not be to new jobs; they may take the form of additional responsibilities in the same job, which may justify a higher-level pay classification.

There is, however, the problem of the employee who has reached the maximum of his range and who is not really capable of assuming greater responsibilities. We can honestly say of such people that they are receiving the top pay for top performance. They can, of course, look forward to sharing in general increases granted by the company or to benefiting from approved adjustments in the pay structure. They can also expect the greater advantages which generally come with years of company service: longer vacations, higher pensions, and more job security.

There are other characteristics of pay structures which are of general interest to managers. Pay relationships between jobs in the company structure, for example, are set by techniques of job evaluation and job grading, and logically do not change over a period of time. On the other hand, labor market pay relationships are influenced by supply and demand, industry composition in the market, collective bargaining relationships, and other factors. As a result, actual market pay relationships may not always resemble the same relationships which have been administratively set under a job evaluation program. Furthermore, pay relationships in a market area will change, and sometimes changes dramatically. Finally, multilocation companies with a single evaluation plan must realize that pay relationships between some jobs may be very different from one labor market area to another.

Such characteristics require flexibility in administering pay structures. Management must keep in close touch with employment and turnover activity, as well as survey data, to make sure that the administratively determined pay relationships conform fairly well to actual relationships in the labor market area. When exceptions exist, they should be made. Any plan with more than 2 percent of the jobs earmarked as exceptions is probably in trouble, but a plan which never has exceptions is probably in trouble also. The essential thing is to make exceptions by exempting them from the system, rather than adjusting the system.

Explaining the Pay Structure

The entire process of setting up and pricing the pay structure is so technical that it does not lend itself readily to simple explanation. However, it is generally only necessary to get across a few basic ideas to employees, such as the following:

1. Pay grades are established to reward employees for different levels of skill, responsibility, and knowledge.
2. The structure is uniform in its nature and administration.
3. The structure is competitive. Usually phrases like "as much or more than . . ." or "equal to . . ." or "the going rate . . ." are sufficiently detailed, provided they are accurate.
4. A range of pay, from minimum to maximum, is established to reward employees for experience and performance.

If the company's policy is to pay average rates with respect to the labor market, it would not necessarily be correct for a supervisor to say that the pay for a given job is equal to rates paid by any company in the area for that job. Pay relationships vary somewhat within each company, and the fact that a company pays the average rate *means* that some other companies are paying less and some are paying more. No company pays more than every other company for every job, and employees tend to quote the higher-pay situation outside their company. Therefore, answers to specific job pay questions must be answered in general terms.

Employee information tends to be less precise than company information; and, as already described, even company information, with all the survey methodology, is far from scientifically accurate. Facts cited by individual employees are usually based on newspaper reports, conversation with friends, a specific job offer, or similar circumstances. Frequently the two companies have quite dissimilar jobs, and the information is sometimes plainly inaccurate. Therefore, supervisors are well advised to discuss serious questions of area pay with the staff to be sure the basis for *their* answers is sound.

INDIVIDUAL PAY DETERMINATION

JOB PRICING, AS INDICATED IN CHAPTER III, IS IMPERSONAL and unconcerned with the question of how well the work is performed. In individual pay administration, on the other hand, management must decide whether all individuals in jobs of the same level should be paid the same and, if not, just how their pay should be determined. Individual pay administration may involve varying rates of base pay or salary, when increases are generally permanent; or bonuses when extra pay for the individual varies directly with output or contribution. Bonus payments will be considered elsewhere. This chapter deals only with variation in individual base pay or salary.

METHODS OF SETTING INDIVIDUAL PAY: SINGLE RATE, INFORMAL, AND AUTOMATIC

There are four basic approaches to determination of individual pay: the single-rate approach, the informal approach, the automatic approach, and the merit approach. Frequently elements of one will be found in the others. For the manager, the merit approach is the more complex and satisfactory, so in this chapter the greatest attention is focused on merit pay administration. First, however, the other approaches will be described here briefly.

Single Rates

It would be a mistake to think that pay differences based on merit are always necessary or desirable within every job classification. Such differences are appropriate only where employee performance can vary significantly on the job. For instance, under a day-work system where the learning time on the job is relatively short, single rates are frequently paid to all employees on jobs of similar difficulty, because everyone is required to work at about the same pace in order to attain standards. In many simple office jobs, also, performance is relatively constant because the routines are so specified or schedules are so set that there is little opportunity for individual effort to affect output materially. To vary pay under such conditions would be to pay a premium for no purpose or penalize without basis. Employees may see variations in jobs like these as favoritism.

The Informal Approach

Whenever supervisors make individual pay decisions without formal guides or controls, they are making these decisions on an informal basis. To be effective, an informal system requires that the supervisor know the person in question well and be in a position to observe him regularly. It also requires a small operation, so that informal decisions can be consistent or at least compatible between groups. Finally, as a minimum, the manager must have basic facts available as to rate of pay, prior increases, and the like. It is usually helpful to maintain at least a tickler file for reviewing pay to make sure that there is some regularity in the frequency of review.

Except under these conditions, it is doubtful whether many managers have sufficient skill, experience, psychic power, and luck to make good pay decisions without guides and controls. Under the pressure of daily operations, most managers will not devote the necessary time to these decisions, nor are they able to obtain and analyze all the information needed in order to decide intelligently.

Under an informal system (which is really little system at all), each manager may have somewhat different standards. Such differences lead to inequities and confusion among employees regarding what is expected of them. Lack of companywide standards may also result in pay decisions influenced by personal favoritism.

Simply requiring the approval of higher-level management on pay decisions does not necessarily overcome these problems. For one thing, managers tend to rationalize their pay recommendations in whatever terms are necessary to gain approval. Furthermore, unless the higher-level managers are informed about the day-to-day performance of the employees who are rated, approval reviews will not necessarily bring about more equitable or logical pay decisions.

The Automatic Approach

Another approach calls for automatic pay changes. This method is the antithesis of the informal approach, for both the amount of the pay increase and the period of review are usually predetermined so that the line supervisor has no discretion in the matter. In jobs where employees need only to gain practice, a knack for the operation, and

INDIVIDUAL PAY

familiarity with the routines in order to attain standard performance, the automatic approach has proved useful and practical. While people will always vary somewhat in their ability to learn and perform a job, the differences in these simple job situations will not always be great enough to justify more complicated approaches. An automatic increase schedule is illustrated in Exhibit 9.

The automatic approach is likely to be applicable not only in lower-level positions but also in situations where a union is not willing to allow management to retain the sole right to advance employees in pay. It is also most likely to occur when management does not do a good job of observing and appraising the performance of employees.

The fact that the automatic approach completely removes individual performance or merit from compensation decisions means that the only incentive an employee really has is to stay with the company long enough for his pay to reach a satisfactory level. Obviously, when this system of pay increases is applied to jobs in which employee

EXHIBIT 9
AN AUTOMATIC INCREASE SCHEDULE

Pay Grade	Starting Rate	Step I	Step II	Step III	Step IV	Step V
1	$1.47	$1.51	$1.56	$1.61	$1.66	$1.71
2	1.58	1.63	1.68	1.73	1.78	1.83
3	1.70	1.75	1.80	1.85	1.90	1.96
4	1.83	1.88	1.93	1.99	2.05	2.11
5	1.96	2.02	2.08	2.14	2.20	2.26
6	2.10	2.16	2.22	2.29	2.36	2.43
7	2.25	2.32	2.39	2.46	2.53	2.60
8	2.42	2.49	2.56	2.64	2.72	2.80
9	2.60	2.68	2.76	2.84	2.92	3.00

Increase to step I three months after date at starting rate.
Increase to higher steps at six-month intervals.
Requests for exceptions must be submitted to plant manager in writing, outlining reasons, with copies to employee and plant personnel manager.

output can vary, it can have serious consequences. The automatic increase policy is also an extremely inflexible approach to wage and salary administration. Once it is adopted, changing it may be difficult even if the economic circumstances affecting company operation change materially.

Actually, in some companies or in some sections of companies, the automatic approach is in effect by reason of practice and precedent if not by policy. This happens where supervisors have with great uniformity granted employees a fixed amount or percentage of increase at regular intervals.

The Merit Rating Approach

If differences in individual performance and output are important to a company, then some basis for compensating employees for these differences should be established. Otherwise, the result may be grievances, unrest, and even turnover among the company's best employees. Merit rating is a management practice designed to gear the pay of employees in the same classification to actual differences in work accomplishments.

Merit rating systems assume that performance can be observed with reasonable accuracy even when it cannot be objectively measured. Thus the first step in a merit rating program is supervisory evaluation of employee performance. This rating is essentially the same process as that used in employee and managerial appraisal programs. Both are concerned with judging performance; it is what is done with the evaluation which often distinguishes the two processes, since merit rating is traditionally used to determine pay increases while appraisal is more and more reserved for training and development.

Merit Rating Techniques

The various types of merit rating techniques which have been developed all have three things in common. First, they can at best only serve to guide managers' thinking about employee performance, potential, or personal qualities. Second, they merely represent an inventory of these factors in a given job situation. This, in itself, does not tell the supervisor how large a merit increase should be granted; nor does it explain why these conditions of performance exist, or how performance might be improved. Third, none of the merit rating techniques are substitutes for managers' judgment, nor are they scientific devices or objective methods. The right technique for a given company is that which best guides the judgment of its managers.

Graphic rating scales. One widely used type of merit rating inventory is the graphic rating scale, illustrated in Exhibit 10, which is quite similar to the technique used in point-evaluation plans. This calls for the supervisor to rate employee performance in terms of prescribed factors or traits. Each trait is defined, and various degrees of each are specified. In rating, the manager selects that degree of each trait which best describes the employee's performance. In some cases, degrees and factors have point weightings so that an overall rating can be obtained.

Those who design the scales face some of the same problems encountered in designing point-evaluation plans. Since job performance is extremely difficult to define and measure, certain traits must be selected to guide the manager's thinking. Just which ones are chosen obviously has an important bearing on the resulting inventory. When applying them in a rating scale, the manager must realize

EXHIBIT 10: A Graphic Rating Scale

Employee's Name: _____ Employee's Classification: _____ Department: _____

Traits	A	B	C	D
QUALITY OF WORK: Consider quality of work produced by employee regardless of quantity.	Often makes mistakes. Work usually unsatisfactory. 1	Part of time maintains passable quality level. 3	Usually does a good job. Makes few errors. 5	Consistently does an excellent job. Few errors. 7
QUANTITY OF WORK: Consider the quantity of work produced by the employee regardless of the quality.	Takes a long time to accomplish little. Output low. 1	Produces reasonably satisfactory volume of work. May need pushing. 3	Produces the required amount of work. Needs no prodding. 5	High production. Exceeds quotas regularly. Completes job quickly. 7
COOPERATIVENESS: Consider the extent to which the employee cooperates with fellow employees and his supervisor.	Does not get along with others. Indifferent. Causes friction and trouble. 1	Fair teamworker. At times inclined to hang back. 2	Gets along satisfactorily with associates. Meets others halfway. 3	Goes out of his way to cooperate with others. 4
DEPENDABILITY: Consider how reliable the employee is and the extent to which you can trust him to carry out your orders conscientiously.	Requires frequent checking or follow-up. Cannot be relied upon without close supervision. 1	Reliable in the performance of most duties. Needs follow-up where assignments are not routine. 2	Carries out instructions adequately. Generally reliable and needs only occasional follow-up. 3	Carries out instructions conscientiously and promptly with excellent results. No need for follow-up. 4
INITIATIVE: Consider the extent to which the employee uses initiative in the performance of his duties and works without constant supervision.	Routine worker. Needs constant supervision—waits to be told. 1	Sometimes at a loss in other than routine situations. Frequent checkup required. 2	Resourceful. Needs little supervision. 3	Performs excellent job with very little supervision. Seeks additional tasks when has time. 4
KNOWLEDGE OF WORK: Consider the employee's knowledge in his particular field; his mastery of all phases of job.	Does not know enough about most phases of his job. 1	More knowledge of some phases of the job would be desirable. 2	Has satisfactory knowledge of practically all phases of his work. 3	Has excellent mastery of all phases of his work. 4

that traits have a different significance in different jobs. For example, persuasive ability is probably the most important single trait for some sales positions, but it typically has little importance for a research scientist. Furthermore, merit rating traits frequently include basic personal qualities as well as those which specifically measure job performance. These traits, such as initiative, dependability, and ability to work well with others, are particularly elusive.

After the factors have been selected, the next task is defining them and establishing degrees within traits. This process raises all the problems already noted in connection with job evaluation factors and degrees. If anything, it is even more difficult to define human traits than to define job characteristics.

Checklists. The checklist is a merit rating inventory which may be especially helpful to supervisors when it is used in connection with graphic rating scales. In the checklist technique, a number of statements are prepared, each relating to employee performance. The supervisor then checks those statements which are descriptive of the work of the employee being rated. Part of a checklist, designed to be used in conjunction with the rating scale in Exhibit 10, is shown in Exhibit 11. Under each factor, the checklist contains a number of questions which examine the employee's performance in far greater detail than the rating scale can. A checklist attempts to pinpoint specific ways in which the employee is doing well or failing to measure up to satisfactory performance. It also indicates in some detail the things a supervisor should consider in judging performance regarding a given factor.

Grouping and ranking. In addition, the manager can roughly evaluate employee performance by grouping or ranking the employees in his group. The easiest grouping technique is slotting employees into broad categories of

EXHIBIT 11
Checklist of Job Performance (Office Positions)

Trait	Assessment		
	Yes	No	Comment

Quality of Work:

1. Have there been specific instances when employee made important mistakes? ___ ___ _____
2. Are mistakes frequently made because of carelessness? ___ ___ _____
3. Are mistakes made because of inexperience or lack of knowledge of the job? ___ ___ _____
4. Does employee learn from mistakes rather than making the same mistakes frequently? ___ ___ _____
5. Is employee's attitude good when mistakes are called to his attention? ___ ___ _____
6. Are mistakes made regularly or just at irregular intervals? ___ ___ _____

Quantity of Work:

1. Is quantity of work as high as should be expected? ___ ___ _____
2. Does quantity of work vary from time to time? ___ ___ _____
3. Does employee do some jobs significantly faster than others? ___ ___ _____
4. Could the employee increase his speed significantly? ___ ___ _____
5. Does employee look for quicker ways of doing things? ___ ___ _____
6. If quantity of work could be increased, could this be done by—
    a. More effort ___ ___ _____
    b. Wasting less time ___ ___ _____
    c. More experience and know-how ___ ___ _____
    d. Closer supervision ___ ___ _____
    e. Other (specify) ___ ___ _____

"excellent," "good," and so forth. Ranking is a simple matter of identifying the best performers in the group and then ranking all the members of it in order down to the poorest. If used thoughtfully, even such crude techniques can help a supervisor to relate pay to performance.

Direct appraisal. Some companies have adopted a system of direct appraisal of how well employees perform their work. When this method is used, an actual list of assigned duties is taken from each job description. Opposite each duty is a space for the manager to assess, first, how important it is in the overall job and, second, how well the employee is performing it. Although this method involves extra clerical work, since a separate appraisal form must be prepared for each job, it goes to the heart of performance evaluation, particularly for pay purposes, by asking in the most straightforward manner how the employee is performing the job.

Critical incident method. While the critical incident method of evaluating employee performance does not lend itself directly to merit rating, it might well be used by supervisors as one technique in the merit rating process. A supervisor can, for instance, maintain a separate folder or data sheet for each employee. Incidents which illustrate either unusual accomplishment or particular job failures can be informally noted, along with the circumstances surrounding them. Similarly, the supervisor can take notes on incidents which illustrate particular characteristics of the employee's work at the time they occur. Such written case histories can be invaluable to the supervisor when preparing merit rating inventories. They can also be very effective when he discusses ratings with employees.

Standards of performance. It is also helpful in making appraisals if the manager decides just what he reasonably expects to be accomplished in each area of responsibility. He will then be in a better position to judge performance by comparing actual accomplishments with the standards he has established. In companies which use written standards of performance, or which practice so-called management by objectives, the manager will have a ready-made means of performance appraisal.

Goal setting. Management by objectives has, in fact, become widely used in recent years. Goal setting begins at top company levels, where overall corporate objectives are established. These are then broken down at successively lower levels into subgoals. Thus each manager and employee participates in establishing specific goals to be achieved during the year, and individual pay adjustments are judged at least in part upon how well each man has accomplished his goals. An example of a simple goal-setting exercise is presented in Exhibit 12.

In a goal-setting or management-by-objectives program, it is assumed that each person will be motivated to perform his assigned duties in a satisfactory manner; the goals established go beyond routine work to specify particular projects which are to be carried out. This method focuses attention on rewards for specific job accomplishment and for results which contribute to the goals of the business as a whole. Goal setting cannot be the sole basis for individual pay determination, but it can be a valuable aid provided that realistic goals are set in the first place, the process does not focus on the demonstrable at the expense of the pertinent activities, it does not become either elaborate or mechanical, and there are business goals which lend themselves to goal-setting projects by individuals.

Increasing the Effectiveness of Ratings

It is obvious that the most excellently conceived and designed merit rating system will not automatically yield

EXHIBIT 12
A GOAL-SETTING EXERCISE

[Adopted from the program of a large pharmaceutical company]

PROJECT TARGETS FOR FISCAL YEAR 19—

Position: Plant Personnel Manager *Incumbent:* R. J. Ricky

	Target Date
1. Conduct community fringe-benefit survey; review with corporate office; submit recommendations.	February 1
2. Bring all office and exempt-position descriptions up to date.	February 1
3. Conduct survey of terminated employees per memo dated November of previous year; present results at April management meeting.	March 1
4. Investigate possibility of middle management plant incentive compensation program; report company practices and prepare written report of feasibility.	July 1
5. Reduce lead time in factory recruiting to seven working days, with no increase in cost per hire.	Fiscal year
6. Develop and recommend management skills training program for foremen.	August 1
7. Conduct management skills program.	October–November

*Approved:*_____

---

valid ratings. The skill with which the techniques are used is as important as the theoretical soundness of the method itself. To the staff specialist, this means that he must provide the line supervisor with technically admirable ones. To the line supervisor, it means that the success of the program depends to a considerable extent upon his skill and effectiveness in rating.

The quality of the merit ratings a manager produces will naturally vary according to the amount of time and thought he invests in the process. His willingness to take pains, in turn, will depend upon what is required of him and whether he sees merit rating as a technique which genuinely helps him as a manager. If he finds that it improves both the performance of his employees and the quality of his personnel actions, he will be strongly motivated to develop skill in rating. There are several ways by which a supervisor can improve the quality of his merit ratings. One is through careful and accurate observation of the employee's actual job performance. Just as the reliability of job evaluation depends upon conscientious job analysis, so the value of personnel evaluation or appraisal depends upon careful observation and analysis of an employee's work. Obviously, ratings based upon casual and infrequent observation can be misleading and unfair.

Managers may also find it useful to tabulate the results of their ratings into summary profiles which can pinpoint possible errors or inconsistencies in rating. By making it easier to compare the rating of one employee with that of another, tabulations also supplement the man-to-rating-scale evaluations.

Another way to improve is simply to rate each employee more than once. The supervisor can rate all his employees, put the ratings aside, and rate all of them again after a two- or three-week period, without reference to the previous results. He may even use an alternative method for his second rating.

Another important requirement is that the manager have a thorough understanding of the rating process. He should know something about merit rating in general, as well as how the system works in his company, what objectives the company has set, what personnel actions are subsequently based upon ratings, and how the system may affect daily operations.

All managers must guard against the natural tendency to reflect their own notions and prejudices in their rating inventories, although most of them undoubtedly rate employees with integrity. Specifically, a manager should try to avoid rating men on the basis of some preconceived idea; subconsciously comparing subordinates with himself; allowing judgments to be influenced by race, creed, or national origin; and permitting one or two incidents to influence unduly the rating of a whole year's performance. He should guard equally against judging potential when judgments of current performance are being made; relying completely on the face that an employee shows him (he may be no better a salesman than a subordinate, or he may be neglecting other duties in order to impress the boss); rating a man unfairly because he is stronger in some characteristics than the manager.

Supervisors can increase the effectiveness of their merit ratings by enlisting the aid of other managers—for instance, by cross-checking their ideas and experiences. Competent staff personnel may also prove helpful in a number of ways. The specialist who has had the opportunity to sit in on rating sessions with many supervisors will have a broader knowledge of merit rating than the line manager who does this work only periodically. The staff member can describe the experiences of other managers and any particular techniques employed by them. He may also help supervisors bring more impartiality into the merit rating session. Finally, he can suggest questions which may clarify points in the rating process, provide information on the objectives, purposes, or details of merit rating, and make constructive suggestions regarding specific problems.

Problems of Merit Rating

Merit rating has not always achieved the objectives which have ben established for it, in spite of the logic of the approach and the considerable research and experience which have been expended in developing its techniques. Managers and employees in many companies have come to dislike merit rating. In fact, this dislike has reached the point in some organizations where true merit rating either has undergone significant modification or has been completely abandoned. What are the primary causes for such failures?

- The measurement of observed performance is not considered accurate enough to serve as a basis for making pay decisions.
- Many merit rating programs have been poorly designed and are technically unsound.
- Many have not been administered properly.
- Sometimes merit rating has been a trick or trap.
- Merit rating objectives have often been in conflict with other basic objectives of the company, of employees, or of individual managers.

Accuracy. Really conclusive research on the accuracy of merit rating has, it is probably fair to say, never been conducted. Empirical tests will probably never be made because of the virtual impossibility of setting standards for measuring accuracy. There is little doubt, however, that even the most formalized merit rating program is a highly subjective process. Human judgments based upon only a partial knowledge of the qualities judged and measured against a very imperfect yardstick are bound to yield results which are in themselves far from perfect.

The fact that merit rating results are not completely objective or scientifically accurate does not, however, justify the conclusion that they are not useful. They must be judged on the basis of possible alternatives and in terms of potential improvement. Managers, from the nature of their responsibilities, judge performance and translate their judgments into personnel actions, including pay decisions as an inherent part of the management process. The question of accuracy is really: How accurate is judgment? The real test of merit rating is whether or not the process results in *improvement* in judgments.

Technical soundness of plan. A number of technical problems concerning merit rating have been encountered and examined at great length in the field of personnel administration. Probably the greatest of these problems is overemphasis on technique. Some staff specialists, faced with problems in merit rating, direct their energies to the things which they understand the best, the technical features of the plan, and lose sight of its broader aspects.

The first technical requirement of a merit plan is that it be a reflection of, or a natural extension of, the normal management practice of the organization. Second, it must be appropriate—not the cleverest or most excellent plan, but one which is suited to the circumstances. Third, it must be usable, which means it must be understandable, believable, and realistic in terms of time demands. Finally, the merit program must meet certain technical tests in terms of form, structure, and methodology.

Poor administration. There is a tendency in most types of programs for management to sustain a high degree of enthusiasm during the design and installation of a program and then to assume that the job is done and the problem is solved. In fact, design and installation represent the beginning and not the end. From the starting date, it typically takes three years of experience before a merit program truly becomes a part of management practice in an enterprise.

Gamesmanship in merit rating. Some merit rating plans have failed to accomplish results simply because the merit rating process has become a game rather than a management process. The game has taken many forms, but basically it involves having the supervisor rate a subordinate's performance and then using his rating to disapprove a recommended increase or actually tell the supervisor what increase he may give. The teams are sometimes staff versus line, sometimes one level of line versus a higher level of line. Almost always, the players concentrate on winning the game at the expense of solving pay problems. Not only are such games silly and expensive, but they frequently assume that the supervisor lacks the ability or the integrity required to supervise.

Conflicts of objectives. Underlying many of the problems of merit rating are some basic conflicts of objectives. One of these is the fact that merit rating is not regarded as equally advantageous by all employees or all managers.

Rewarding higher performance with higher pay is important and beneficial to employees whose performance is actually better than average; to the company, which gains through lower unit costs; and to those managers who thereby promote more efficient operations. However, gearing pay to performance is contrary to the self-interest of others. For instance, employees who perform below average will object to merit rating because they may receive less pay than they would otherwise. In addition, supervisors may oppose the process because they lack the time and skill necessary to carry out their responsibilities under a merit rating program, because they are uncomfortable with appraisal, because they prefer a personalized approach, or for other reasons.

Another basic conflict of objectives, which seems to be of far greater concern to academic researchers than to managers or employees, is the fact that merit rating is essentially an authoritarian procedure. Some object to the fact that managers seem to be "playing God" when they rate employees, particularly when ratings are based on personal characteristics. Those who fear merit rating for this reason, however, overlook the fact that business must always be authoritarian to some extent and that managers must, in one way or another, evaluate the performance of their subordinates and take appropriate action as a result. Merit rating is merely one technique which attempts to improve this process and make it more objective. Anyone who is inclined to be distressed when faced with the responsibility of judging the business worth of another person cannot be a business manager, for this is an essential management responsibility and cannot be evaded.

It is interesting that while some academic authorities oppose merit rating because it is too authoritarian, managers are sometimes opposed to merit rating because it restricts their absolute authority. Supervisors who so contend are correct. Merit rating is a company system intended to both guide and control managers. While the emphasis should always be on guiding them, the element of control is also present. Top management cannot completely delegate such an important function without providing standards to guide lower-level management.

Another conflict involves the perfunctory manner in which merit rating is sometimes applied. In some companies, no one really pays any attention to it; forms are completed, filed, and forgotten. The process becomes mere routine and serves no purpose for the employee, the company, or the supervisor. Other companies seem to pay great attention to their merit rating program on the surface but disregard it in practice by granting automatic raises and allowing all employees to get to the top of their pay grades within a fairly standard period of time. Under such conditions, merit rating certainly becomes a matter of empty form.

The most important conflict of objectives involves basic purpose. Even in companies where pay reviews are centrally conducted and rigidly tied to merit rating inventories, the process can become mechanical because managers tend to decide first what pay increases they want to give and then figure out what type of merit rating they must submit in order to justify the increase. While it is easy to criticize line managers who engage in such practices, it must also be recognized that this sometimes happens because the basic objectives of performance review are in direct conflict with those of pay review, making it impossible to tie wages solely to merit rating. This fundamental conflict of purpose between performance evaluation and personnel actions is really at the heart of many of the problems which face merit rating.

USE OF THE MERIT RATING PROCESS

In some companies the supervisor is required to justify any merit increase by means of the merit rating inventory. In other firms, the same end is accomplished by a central auditing of recommended pay changes with the use of merit inventory forms which have been prepared in advance. In either case, an attempt is made to establish a direct relationship between the recommended pay increase and the merit rating results. While this is a logical conclusion of the basic objective of tying the pay within ranges to the individual employee's performance on the job, such a rigid relationship assumes that (1) performance is the only factor which should be considered in determining an individual employee's pay within pay ranges; (2) evaluation by merit rating is designed only to determine merit increases; and (3) evaluation by merit rating is an extremely accurate process.

Actual experience with merit rating, however, indicates that none of these assumptions is correct.

A Modified Merit Rating Approach

The traditional approach to merit rating can be modified without losing the basic objective of relating individual pay within pay ranges to individual performance. The modified merit rating approach first involves the recognition that the preparation of the merit rating inventory is essentially an appraisal process. This appraisal or performance review process is a management technique which is designed to crystallize the manager's knowledge of employee performance and improve his judgment of it.

Exhibit 13 shows the proper relationship between performance review and compensation review. The performance review is the cornerstone of management actions designed to utilize the employee resources of the company more fully. It has a number of important purposes; helping to make more realistic pay decisions is only one of them. At the same time, employee performance is only one of the basic factors that managers must consider in making merit pay decisions.

These statements suggest a new emphasis in the preparation of merit rating inventories, or in otherwise evaluating individual employee performance. They also call attention to the need for a broader look at individual merit pay decisions through the consideration of other

EXHIBIT 13
Relationship Between Performance Review and Compensation Review

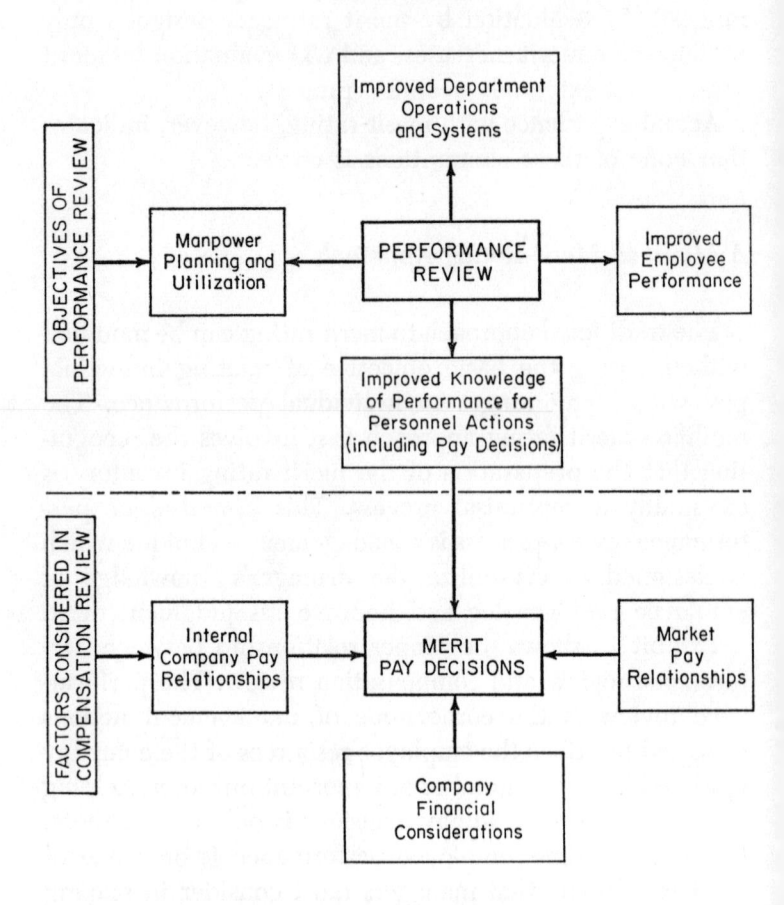

OBJECTIVES OF PERFORMANCE REVIEW:
- Manpower Planning and Utilization
- Improved Department Operations and Systems
- Improved Employee Performance
- Improved Knowledge of Performance for Personnel Actions (including Pay Decisions)

All connected to central box: **PERFORMANCE REVIEW**

FACTORS CONSIDERED IN COMPENSATION REVIEW:
- Internal Company Pay Relationships
- Market Pay Relationships
- Company Financial Considerations
- (Improved Knowledge of Performance for Personnel Actions)

All connected to central box: **MERIT PAY DECISIONS**

essential factors. Finally, the close connection between performance review and compensation review demonstrates the desirability of physically separating the two processes. Physical separation does not, of course, imply that performance should not be considered in pay decisions. The greater knowledge that the manager obtains through appraisal should be an important factor in these decisions.

Objectives of Performance Review

Under the modified approach to merit rating, the manager is able to concentrate more objectively on employee performance. He need not be concerned about the fact that an honest appraisal may sometimes result in an unrealistic pay decision, as is the case in the traditional approach.

Improved employee performance. Probably the most important single purpose of review is to improve the performance of individual employees. Specifically, the performance review process may include the following:

1. Observation of employee performance.
2. Comparison of work actually done with job duties assigned.
3. Measurement of performance by merit rating factors, preparation of the merit rating inventory.
4. Use of the inventory to identify the two or three strongest traits demonstrated by the employee. By focusing on the most pertinent points, this makes it easier for the supervisor to give the employee credit for his accomplishments and to explore the possibility of capitalizing further upon them.
5. Identification of the two or three areas in which the employee needs the greatest improvement.
6. Analysis of these areas to determine what the supervisor should do in order to help the employee improve.
7. Re-examination of these areas to determine what the employee himself should do in order to improve.

This performance review process helps not only the employee who is appraised but also the manager who does the appraising. The process of studying job duties, setting work standards, and observing employee performance is bound to increase the supervisor's knowledge of his operations and his understanding of the problems involved. The observation of performance will help him see what obstacles prevent his employees from doing their best work. Similarly, it may reveal ways in which the manager himself can become a more effective supervisor.

Determining training needs. Well-executed performance reviews can play a major role in group training efforts. What better procedure could be evolved to determine training needs than to have each supervisor analyze the performance of his employees and record, for staff use, the developmental opportunities of each person? With the information he provides, long-range training needs can be identified and company training programs developed.

Improved department operations. Managers can also use the performance review directly to improve operations. For example, it can suggest how job duties should be reassigned to take advantage of employees' strengths, to minimize their weaknesses, and to correct internal job placement. The appraisal may also pinpoint bottlenecks which prevent effective operations, or may indicate improvements which could be made in methods, procedures, department layout, and so forth.

Manpower inventory. Of course, the performance review process provides useful inventories of manpower skills. These written records of supervisory appraisal, submitted at the time when the actual analysis of employee performance is conducted, can be valuable to future supervisors, either when the employee is promoted or when a new man takes over the operation of the department. From the broader point of view, the manpower inventory can be of material assistance in managerial planning. By matching the skills and abilities of the employees within the group against planned developments, the manager is in a better position to provide for orderly growth or change.

Improved personnel actions. The final objective of performance review is to crystallize managerial knowledge and understanding of employee performance in order to make more realistic and equitable personnel decisions. This includes the identification of employees for promotion purposes, as well as the reassignment of employees within the operating unit to utilize their skills in a better way. Merit rating inventories may also be the basis for disciplinary action, or they may serve to guide managers in scheduling layoffs when ability and performance are part of the employment-security policy.

Pay Decisions in Perspective

Pay decisions must be viewed in the proper perspective as regards the overall objectives of performance review. Performance cannot be the only factor considered in making merit pay decisions, for the following reasons.

1. If a company were to tie merit increases rigidly to performance, it would be saying to its employees that pay always improves when performance improves. In practice, however, a formalized wage and salary program sets a maximum value on each job. If these maximums are enforced, the employee who has reached the top and still improves his performance cannot have his pay increased.

2. While tested merit rating techniques which are carried out by trained and experienced raters can bring reasonable results, it would be a mistake to consider them so accurate that each additional improvement in job performance is worth equal increments in pay.

3. If we were to tie merit increases inflexibly to per-

formance, it would mean that when performance declined, an employee would automatically have his pay cut. In most cases, however, this is not considered practical unless performance declines to the point where disciplinary action is absolutely necessary.

4. It may be necessary to grant an employee an increase because of pay inequities even though such an increase is not justified on the grounds of improved performance.

5. Because of financial considerations, the company may not be able to grant the increases justified by performance.

To sum up, then, managers must consider many factors in deciding so-called merit increases, such as—

- *The employee performance review.*
- *Company pay relationships*, which include:
  1. The individual employee's pay history.
  2. The employee's present position within his pay range.
  3. The experience the employee has had in his present position.
  4. The period of time since the employee's last increase.
  5. The amount of the previous increase.
  6. The pay relationships within the supervisor's department.
  7. The levels of pay received by employees doing similar work in other departments.
- *Labor market considerations*, which include:
  1. Pay experience with newly hired employees.
  2. The pay received by employees doing similar work in other companies in the labor market area.
- *Operating considerations*, which include:
  1. The importance of the work being done.
  2. The financial budget which has been assigned by the company for merit rating purposes.

Each of these factors strongly influences individual pay decisions. They are frequently in conflict in the sense that if each were considered separately, different decisions might result. When such conflicts arise, some compromise must be reflected in pay decisions, because none of these factors can be neglected for long.

It is also significant that the individual supervisor cannot independently judge the importance of each of the forces affecting individual pay decisions and decide how much influence it is to have. Some factors, such as employee performance, must be determined exclusively by the manager. He must, however, rely on the staff for other information such as companywide pay relations and market area comparisons of employee earnings. Still other factors, such as the merit rating budget, are the responsibility of top management.

SALARY PLANNING

Individual pay decisions based on merit thus involve a number of factors. The difficult job is to identify the pertinent factors, give them due consideration, and arrive at proper pay decisions. Many companies have introduced formal programs to assist in this process. Even where there is no formal system, many managers have devised their own methods to help meet their basic pay responsibilities. Salary planning is one method used to accomplish these objectives.

Need for Planning

To relate pay to performance in a realistic manner, give weight to other considerations, and do this in a consistent manner for all employees requires some systematic planning approach. There is also a great need for salary planning because of the amount of money involved. Whether or not an employee is classified in one pay grade or the next highest generally involves a difference of something like 10 percent. However, within-grade progressions are generally from 30 to 60 percent, so that three to six times as much money is involved as in the determination of the proper classifications.

Another reason for salary planning is the greater number of persons who are involved in making the merit rating decisions. Generally, even in a decentralized organization, there are only a limited number of people responsible for the final decisions relating to pay classifications, and they need only consider the analysis of job duties and the job evaluation yardstick. In determining merit increases, however, the decision making is delegated to the individual supervisors. People—and there are many of them—must consider not only the performance of duties, but also market-pay relationships, the financial budget provided for them, the individual pay history of each employee, and other information which was discussed in the previous section.

Elements of Planning

While salary planning may mean many things to many people, it should at least include: (1) a broad enough base of information for the manager to be able to consider the elements which should go into the determination of merit increases; (2) preplanning of increases—the supervisor should plan both the amount and the time of increase for all employees within his group for a full year's period; (3) counseling by staff specialists to assist the manager in interpreting the complex data involved in pay decisions and to insure that the various procedures and policies of the company have been observed.

The type of information required for effective salary planning varies a great deal, of course, depending upon the types of jobs which are being considered. Basically, it includes the kind of data illustrated in Exhibit 14, together with some facts relating to internal pay relationships, and at least bench-mark information on pay relationships with competing companies. Summary data can be reduced to a salary-analysis worksheet such as the one in Exhibit 14, and supplemental information on pay histories and competition data can be prepared separately for more detailed examination.

This type of salary planning has been adopted in a number of companies. They have found from experience that it has a number of distinct advantages:

1. The supervisor brings consistency and objectivity into his determination of merit increases by planning them for all employees at the same time.

2. This preplanning is the only efficient way of considering all relevant information. If the supervisor had to consider all the data on each employee when a pay raise for him came up for review, he would be forced to go through the same process and much the same information many times during the year.

3. Preplanning is the only realistic manner of estimating merit budgets. The preplanning of merit increases allows management to predict the impact of these increases on operating costs.

4. Preplanning of increases assures equal treatment for all employees regardless of what time of the year their pay reviews are due. Unless this is done, some employees may suffer because of operating circumstances or other conditions which may influence management's willingness to grant increases.

EXHIBIT 14
SALARY PLANNING SHEET

Department: _____ Supervisor: _____ Budget $: _____

Position	Name	Current Salary	Pay Grade	Band Position	Total Percent Increase from 1/1/19—	Last Increase Amount Percent Date	Perf. Rate	Planned Increase Amount Percent Date

Total Preplanning _____ Average Preplanning _____ Total _____
Total After _____ Average After _____ Variance _____

5. Preplanning of merit increases by all supervisors within a company or operating unit insures that employees as a group are being treated in a consistent manner compared with other groups.

6. Careful preplanning of this type can make possible a true delegation of merit pay decision making to the lowest levels of supervision. Similarly, preplanning can facilitate approval procedures.

Salary planning should never become a rigid and inflexible instrument for pay decisions. Circumstances often change during the course of a year. An employee may actually perform more efficiently than was anticipated, in which case management may want to give him a somewhat higher merit increase when his actual review date occurs. Experience has shown, however, that these changes do not occur frequently. Performance within a given job situation depends on basic personal qualities such as intelligence, self-motivation, energy, and attitude, and these qualities generally do not change dramatically in a year's time unless the work environment also changes.

Explaining Pay Decisions to Employees

The basic objective of merit rating cannot be accomplished unless the supervisor can explain his decisions adequately to employees. Under the modified approach, of course, he will not discuss pay increases exclusively in terms of performance. He will point out to employees that performance, while a basic consideration, is only one of the factors he has to consider in making individual pay decisions.

Some managers rebel against the idea of having to explain a raise. Employees, however, are interested in getting not just any raise but the raise they think they are entitled to, and it is the task of the manager to explain why he decided on the particular amount he did.

Traditionally, supervisors have discussed both the employee's performance and the resulting pay increase at the same time, in a session commonly called the "post-merit rating interview." However, if there is logic in physically separating performance review from compensation review, then it seems equally logical to discuss performance and pay increases at separate times. Unless this is done, consideration of the merit pay increase is likely to dominate the interview.

Ideally, the manager discusses performance with each of his subordinates whenever the appropriate circumstances warrant it throughout the year. Any conferences following the periodic performance review will thus be primarily directed toward ways in which the employee's work might be further improved. If these review sessions are handled well, and the supervisor has been working with his subordinates throughout the year, the groundwork for the discussion of the merit pay increase will already have been established. This conference can then deal primarily with why the supervisor arrived at the particular amount of increase.

Explaining the amount of a raise is not always an easy matter, particularly if the supervisor has had to judge a number of conflicting factors in arriving at his decision. Because of this, and because of the importance of this interview, the manager should prepare for it by reviewing the facts which led to the merit pay decision. He also should attempt to anticipate employee reactions to his explanation to the fullest extent possible and prepare himself accordingly. What is actually said will, of course, vary with each session. In all cases, however, the supervisor should make sure that the employee understands just how the decisions are reached and what factors (including

INDIVIDUAL PAY

performance) were considered. The employee should then have an opportunity to comment on the decision—free from fear of reprisal.

Just how well the employee accepts the pay decision will, of course, depend partly on the size of the increase. It will also depend upon whether he is impressed by the manager's thoughtfulness and thoroughness in making the decision. Finally, the employee's attitude will be guided to some extent by his understanding of the company merit rating program.

CHAPTER V

ADMINISTRATION OF THE PAY PROGRAM

EFFECTIVE ADMINISTRATION OF THE PAY PROGRAM MUST be exercised within a framework which includes company policies, laws governing wage and salary administration, collective bargaining contracts, ground rules designed to guide specific decisions, and various controls established by management. These vital aspects of pay administration must be well understood by managers if the pay problems of the business are to be resolved and company goals and objectives achieved.

POLICIES, LAWS, AND COLLECTIVE BARGAINING AGREEMENTS

In combination, company compensation policies, state and Federal laws relating to compensation, and collective bargaining agreements represent what must be regarded as the "laws" governing pay actions. Of course, it is important to follow these laws without exception. Also important is the manner in which they are interpreted and explained by supervisors, for it is this which determines what the laws mean in specific cases, or what employees think they mean.

Wage and Salary Policies

Since the techniques of the compensation program should essentially be extensions of company policies, intelligent use of these techniques requires an understanding of the policies themselves. Salary policy manuals frequently are thick volumes. In actual fact, there are not more than two dozen possible pay policy questions and only six crucial ones.

One important matter is the general policy of the company with respect to compensation levels. As demonstrated in Chapter IV, in any labor market or group of markets, an employer has some discretion in setting pay levels. They may be geared to the average pay or to pay above or below average levels, depending on the nature of the markets and the level of the jobs.

Another important policy matter is the question of delegation of authority. First, management must set the level in the line organization at which pay decisions are essentially made. As Exhibit 15 illustrates, one company's thinking on this issue is that authority should be delegated to the immediate supervisor; approval comes at the next higher level, and above that there is only general and informational review. Many companies follow other systems, however.

A second aspect of the delegation question involves the relative authority vested in staff and line. Ideally, according to management theory, the line supervisor would have full authority. However, since such a policy would mean that final decisions with respect to position descriptions, job evaluations, and individual pay increases would be

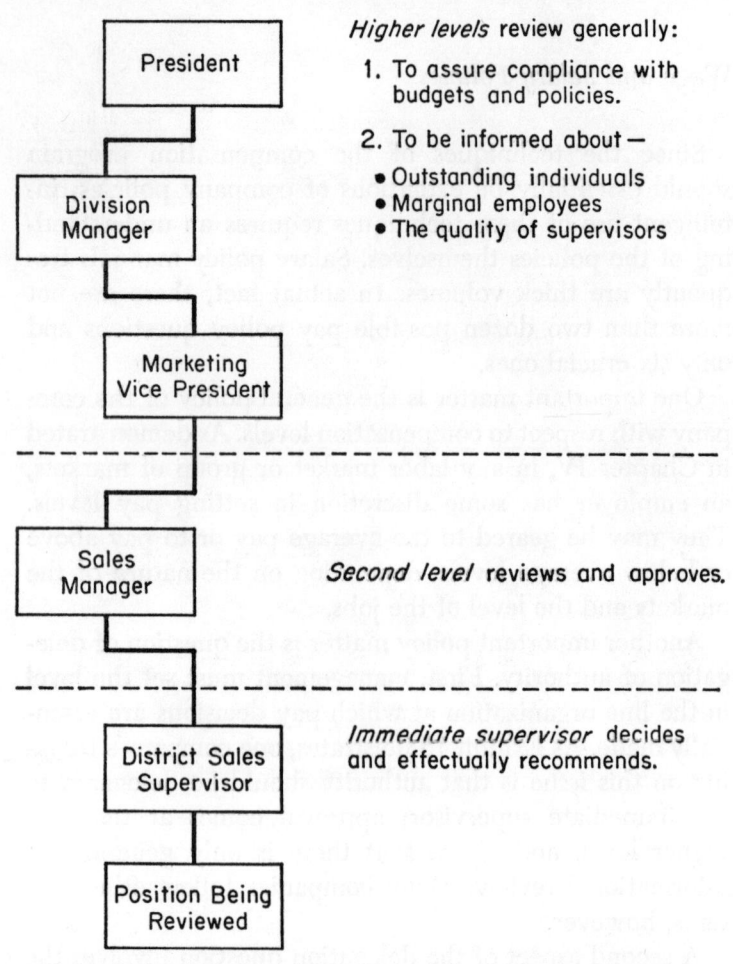

EXHIBIT 15
ONE COMPANY'S POLICY ON DELEGATION

```
┌──────────────┐
│  President   │
└──────┬───────┘
       │
┌──────┴───────┐
│   Division   │
│   Manager    │
└──────┬───────┘
       │
┌──────┴───────┐
│  Marketing   │
│Vice President│
└──────┬───────┘
- - - -│- - - - - - - - - - - - - - -
┌──────┴───────┐
│    Sales     │
│   Manager    │
└──────┬───────┘
- - - -│- - - - - - - - - - - - - - -
┌──────┴───────┐
│District Sales│
│  Supervisor  │
└──────┬───────┘
       │
┌──────┴───────┐
│Position Being│
│   Reviewed   │
└──────────────┘
```

Higher levels review generally:

1. To assure compliance with budgets and policies.
2. To be informed about —
   - Outstanding individuals
   - Marginal employees
   - The quality of supervisors

Second level reviews and approves.

Immediate supervisor decides and effectually recommends.

made by line supervisors, this ideal is seldom achieved in practice.

The general philosophy of the company with respect to individual pay progress is a third policy area. This entails more than a question of merit increases based upon performance; it also involves company attitudes toward the pay progress of employees, the sharing of company progress, and improvement in real income.

Other policy questions concern communications between management and employees about the details of the salary administration program. Specifically, should employees be shown position descriptions? Should they know the minimum and the maximum of their pay range? Should the basis of pay increases be described? Should information be given to employees on the company pay structure as compared with others in the labor markets?

A fifth vital policy area refers to use of the pay program. For one thing, what is the company's attitude with respect to keeping the program up to date? This can involve such details as requiring that position descriptions always reflect current assignments of responsibility and such broader questions as how often, how thoroughly, the pay structure will be reviewed. A second general question which concerns the use of the program is tied up with basic management philosophy: Is the program to be incorporated as a management method and, therefore, a natural reflection of management practices, or is it to be a personnel technique to meet specific types of problem situations? Finally, the use of the program involves a matter of organizational discipline. One company has dealt directly with this question by stating in its salary administration manual:

> Every supervisor is required to use the techniques and methods of this program at all times. This means, for instance, that in thinking about the relative value of all jobs we think in terms of our job evaluation plan and the factors identified in that plan. It means that all use the merit increase schedule as a guide.
>
> Most sets of methods or techniques are imperfect. After careful study, however, management decided those out-

lined in this manual were the methods and techniques which were most appropriate for our company. It is a management decision that they should be used.

If you have a better technique or method, let us hear about it. You can be sure that it will be carefully considered. If, indeed, it turns out to be better, then we will incorporate that suggestion and everyone will be required to use it.

A final policy question involves the form of compensation—that is, how much of his total compensation the employee should get in salary, extra compensation, insured benefits, pay for time not worked, and indirect benefits.

These may not be all the possible policy questions concerning wage and salary administration, but they are the crucial ones. One way of testing the effectiveness of a pay program is to determine the degree to which supervisors really understand the company's policies on these matters. The reader might pause here to check whether he himself is thoroughly familiar with his own company's policies.

Just how well managers do understand such company policy matters depends upon how well these policies and the thinking behind them are communicated. One effective way of accomplishing this is simply to put them in writing. A study of compensation policies in 100 leading companies revealed that 67 of the companies had no written policies on compensation and that, in the judgment of the surveyors, 25 of the 33 written statements were so general as to be useless from the standpoint of communicating to individual supervisors or to the employees the company's thinking on essential policy matters. Actually, the crucial questions outlined in the preceding paragraphs could be covered in a few pages.

Even when policies are written out, they are only statements of intentions and the conscience of the company.

It is the day-to-day interpretations that give body, substance, and meaning to policies just as court decisions give body and meaning to written laws. Because of this, some companies have supplemented written policy statements by more detailed memoranda discussing intent or giving examples of applications. Formal meetings designed to explain both the policies and the basic thinking behind them and to describe specific applications also can be most helpful. Counseling sessions, either by higher-level managers or by staff personnel, provide still another method.

In the last analysis, however, policies are primarily communicated by the actions of management. If the supervisor reads that it is the company's policy to reward performance by greater pay but sees his supervisor granting increases on a different basis, he will tend to follow the leader. The whole general climate and the obvious vitality of the business, together with higher-level management decisions, communicate the basic attitude of the company on these policy matters.

Some companies, in enthusiastic pursuit of consistency, spell out compensation policies and practices in such detail that they become rules rather than guides. Such rigidity will, of course, take the place of policy interpretation and deprive managers of the decision-making role altogether. If adequately policed, this course assures conformity, but it is not well calculated to solve pay problems.

Legal Requirements

As stated, in addition to the policies of the company, a number of laws directly affect wage and salary decisions. While the advice of legal counsel is required to answer specific questions of law, there are certain basic legal requirements which should be known to all who are involved in the administration of wage and salary programs. A single instance in which one of the laws is violated by an uninformed supervisor can result in a substantial fine, a penalty payment, the loss of government business, or court action.

The more important laws covering wage payment are these:

1. *Overtime payments.* The Fair Labor Standards Act requires that employees who are not exempt from the Act be paid time and one-half for all work over 40 hours per week. This law, with subsequent administrative decisions, spells out in great detail the conditions which must be met in order for an employee to be exempt from the provisions of the Act. The supervisor should recognize that the company has no discretion here; he must check carefully with the personnel staff and with legal counsel, if necessary, with respect to the status of any questionable position.

2. *Minimum wages.* There are also legal requirements as to the minimum wages which can be paid an employee. Compliance with this law is generally a matter of companywide practice. Supervisors, however, should not only be cognizant of the law but recognize the impact of minimum wages upon pay differentials within the company.

3. *Rates of pay for government contractors.* The Walsh-Healy Act requires employers who engage in certain types of government contract work to pay the "going rates" of the areas in which the work is performed and to pay overtime for work in excess of eight hours a day. Failure to meet this requirement generally can involve the company in considerable difficulties.

4. *Antidiscrimination laws.* Discrimination with respect to pay because of an employee's race, color, creed, or sex

has always been contrary to good business practice or social justice; it is now prohibited by law.

Collective Bargaining Requirements

The National Labor Relations Act requires employers to bargain in good faith with certified union representatives on all matters relating to "wages and conditions of work." This means that employers must negotiate with union representatives concerning not only the pay of employees but also all techniques, practices, and procedures which affect the earnings of any employee. Thus, among organized employees, the collective bargaining agreement in effect represents a policy guide for supervisors. Management can be certain that its actions will be closely audited by union stewards.

Union attitudes. Labor leaders generally have not favored the techniques associated with a formal wage and salary program. They have usually opposed job evaluation specifically, and they almost invariably object to merit rating programs which gear earnings to management judgments of work performance.

The major objection raised by union leaders is that the techniques of wage and salary administration are a substitute for collective bargaining. They recognize, for instance, that if job evaluation guides the thinking of managers and union leaders, the determination of individual pay relationships is largely removed from collective bargaining. In addition, they sometimes see a formal plan as primarily a management guide. They are reluctant to accept unilateral management judgments—particularly if these judgments are based on a system which, in the opinion of the union leaders, does not necessarily guarantee more logical results than those which could be obtained through the give-and-take of collective bargaining. Finally, unions have criticized some pay techniques on the basis that they are too complicated for workers to understand.

Unions are sometimes frank to say they suspect that some of the methods used in formal wage and salary administration programs are really management tricks rather than management techniques. They fear that some of the more intricate procedures represent a complicated and confusing cloak to hide continuing discriminatory practices and that none of these plans was engineered or designed for the benefit of employees.

In some long-established and mature collective bargaining relationships, however, unions have participated with management in the development and administration of job evaluation programs. Union leaders have actually viewed the techniques, not only as a valuable management-labor guide for reaching agreement but also as a means of explaining the results of these agreements to their members. In other situations, unions have seen the various techniques as a method of getting more for workers. For instance, some have found it to their advantage to bargain for upgradings through job evaluation, rather than to bargain on the basis of overall job worth. In this way, they can use each factor judgment under the evaluation plan as a means of achieving upgrading. Also, during periods of government wage controls, unions have accepted job evaluation programs as a necessary means of getting government approval for pay increases.

Collective bargaining guides. Where a collective bargaining agreement exists, supervisors must exercise the same care in interpreting and applying this agreement as they would company policies. While the administration of a labor agreement is a highly specialized area, experience has shown that the following points are particularly important:

1. Management must take great care in assigning employees to work in their proper pay classifications.
2. Where job assignments change, the new position should be re-evaluated promptly.
3. Management must thoroughly understand the procedures of collective bargaining administration. For instance, must a new position be discussed with the union representatives before it is established?
4. The pay progression practices in the collective bargaining contract must be strictly followed.
5. Managers at all levels should be familiar with the provisions of the grievance system, should know which pay questions are subject to grievance handling, and should understand how pay grievances are processed.
6. Managers must be alert to the possibility of "whipsawing." One request for a change in pay grade, though in itself not significant, can be the basis for gaining upgradings for many other positions.

GROUND RULES FOR PAY ADMINISTRATION

Ground rules refer to those guides which pertain to salary actions other than pay increases within pay ranges. In some firms, ground rules are in written form. Elsewhere they may be only precedents, informal communications from higher-level management, or experience gained by past practice. Some of the principal areas requiring ground rules are outlined briefly below.

Hiring Rates of Pay

It is generally sound practice to hire new employees at or near the minimum of the pay range which has been established for the job, assuming the pay structure fits realistically into the labor market. In theory, applicants with minimum experience qualifications should be hired at the bottom of the pay range; those with greater experience at a higher rate.

If new employees are hired much above the lower third of the pay range, there will be little opportunity for increases as they learned the company's operations and improved their performance. Furthermore, hiring new employees high in the range may create inequities: applicants who seem better qualified during the employment process may not turn out to be truly superior to those already on the payroll.

A limited amount of unfavorable employment experience may lead a supervisor to think that the company pay structure is inadequate. Employment experience is, in fact, one of the most practical tests of the adequacy of a company's pay structure. However, it is important to recognize that success in employment depends on a number of critical factors, including—

- Adequacy of the pay structure.
- Correctness of pay classification.
- Hiring range established within pay range.
- Labor availability.
- Employment requirements.
- Recruiting requirements.
- Screening techniques.
- Number of employees being recruited.
- Elapsed time permitted for hiring.

All of these factors are crucial to the employment process. For example, unnecessarily high employment requirements are frequently the obstacle to effective recruiting. Or the recruiting techniques themselves may be the problem; in the labor shortages of recent years, imaginative and aggressive recruiting methods are frequently not only appropriate but actually justifiable from the cost point of view. As a rule of thumb, $1 per year more in starting pay is the cost equivalent of $5 in extra recruiting cost.

There are two special cases which frequently cause difficulty with respect to the appropriate hiring rate. The first is the situation where the duties to be performed are somewhat indefinite, so that the appropriate classification must also be uncertain. Such a problem is sometimes caused by actual uncertainties in operations—the uncertain impact of a new product, for example, or the effect of computer technology. Frequently, however, the question to ask is this: If the supervisor cannot determine what work must be assigned to the new employee, how can he be sure that he needs a new employee?

The second difficult hiring situation involves jobs with rapidly emerging responsibilities. Typical might be the case of the foreman who is hired to run a department of three persons which, within months, may become a department of 300. Usually, the correct course here is to classify the job according to the situation as it now exists and to set the hiring rate in relation to the job as it is expected to become. In fact, it frequently takes a better man, with a higher rate of pay, to build an organization than to run an organization.

Amount of Merit Increases

The methods used and the principles involved in merit increase policy and progression within range have already been discussed. In addition, however, there are usually some ground rules concerning the minimum and maximum merit increases which are appropriate.

Generally speaking, for instance, it is not considered wise to grant an increase of much less than 3 percent for production and office employees, 5 percent for administrative supervisors and technical employees, and 7 percent for management and professional employees. The reasons are simple. First, it is doubtful whether a supervisor can judge merit and the other factors which must be considered so finely as to justify increases smaller than these amounts. Furthermore, to the employees, such increases after taxes may represent only nominal amounts which do not motivate them to improve performance and may actually have a negative effect on their attitudes.

In considering minimum increases, supervisors should bear in mind that pay progress is a function of amount of increase and frequency of increase. Where significant merit increases cannot be justified for an employee, it is probably wiser to delay the period of increase so that the small increases described are avoided. Sometimes imaginative thinking can solve the problem of the minimum merit increase. For example, one such method which not only eliminates this problem but has other employee relations advantages, is the "lump sum" merit increase. Under this plan an employee is advanced the whole annual amount of the merit increase: An employee who is earning $12,000 per year and is eligible for a 5 percent increase on the first of the year would receive a $600 payment and then continue to receive $1,000 per month in salary for the balance of the year. On the first of the following year his pay would go to $1,100. At this time he might receive another lump sum merit increase.

The maximum limitations on merit increases are more difficult to determine. Theoretically, there should be no limit to an individual's salary progress except the limit of his own performance improvement. As a practical matter, however, increases in excess of 20 percent should be carefully reviewed from the point of view of budget, motivation, and effect on attitudes of others. Again, in such situations a supervisor should bear in mind the timing of raises. If performance progress is extraordinary, to the point where unusually large merit increases seem justified, it might be wiser to grant smaller increases more frequently. As a practical matter, under this approach the increases would more closely match the actual progress of the individual.

The structure itself, and any changes in that structure, also impose ground rules affecting the amount of merit increases. Any merit increase which is less in percentage than an adjustment in the pay structure since the employee's last increase represents, in effect, a decline in pay. The supervisor must also consider the amount of time that would transpire before the employee would reach the top of his range as a result of different rates of pay progress. Exhibit 16 shows the number of years that it would take under given conditions of pay structure, rate of structure increase, and rate of merit increases.

EXHIBIT 16
Years to Range Maximum

Percent Spread Within Range	\multicolumn{5}{c}{Years to Go from Minimum of Range to Maximum If Structure Advances 3 Percent per Year and Average Annual Merit Increase (as a Percent) Is:}
	4	6	8	10	12
20	17	6	4	3	2
30	23	8	5	4	3
40	37	13	8	6	4

Frequency of Merit Review

Ideally, the frequency of consideration for merit increases should be determined by the level of an employee's job and the length of time he has been on it. Job level is a factor because demonstrable improvements in performance take longer to observe in higher-level jobs. Employees in higher pay grades, therefore, should be reviewed less frequently than those in lower jobs. Time on the job should be considered in determining the intervals of merit review because performance progress generally follows the pattern of a learning curve. An employee learns more rapidly during his first months on a new job; his rate of improvement then typically slows down very markedly, and after a while performance does not increase at all. Thus employees should receive more frequent reviews when they are new on a job, and the interval should become less frequent with time. As an illustration of how these principles may be translated into concrete guides, Exhibit 17 presents the merit review schedule of one company.

EXHIBIT 17
INTERVALS BETWEEN CONSIDERATION FOR MERIT INCREASES

Pay Grade	Less than 1 Year	1–3 Years	3–10 Years	Over 10 Years
1–8	3	6	12	12
9–16	6	12	12	18
17–30	12	12	18	24
Over 30	12	18	24	36

Months Between Merit Reviews If Employee Has Been on Current Job

Promotional Increases

Promotion can logically be defined as a move from a job in one pay grade to a job in a higher pay grade. It follows that an employee should receive a pay increase when he is promoted; otherwise he would be asked to do more without receiving more.

Sometimes a promotional increase is deferred until the

employee has proved himself in the new job. Such a practice is inequitable in the sense that it would not be followed if an employee were recruited for the job from the outside. Furthermore, it is illogical in the sense that the company has better opportunities for screening men inside than it does men outside. Deferment of the increase, since it reflects a doubt as to the capability of the individual on the new job, may actually undermine the employee's self-confidence.

In determining how much of a promotional increase should be granted, the supervisor must consider a number of factors: the magnitude of the promotion, the employee's position within range in the new position, and the pay progress the employee might reasonably have received through merit increases if he had not received a promotion.

The ground rules one company has established for promotional increases take all these factors into consideration:

1. Generally speaking, pay progress of a promoted employee should be greater than it would most likely have been if he were not promoted.
2. The salary of the incumbent should be raised to at least the minimum of the pay level of his new position.
3. The promotional increase should in no case be less than 5 percent.
4. When a promotion of more than one pay grade is involved, the minimum promotional increase should be 3 percent per pay grade.
5. Promotional increases should never exceed 20 percent. In the event that a greater increase is required to satisfy one of the other ground rules, the matter must be referred to the personnel policy committee and data must be supplied *with respect to compensation and selection.*

Frequently, promotions do not involve a direct move to

a distinctly different job with a higher pay grade. Rather, they reflect emerging job duties or a series of additional assignments over a period of time. No one of these changed duties may in itself warrant a change in pay classification, but when they are accumulated over a period of time a promotion results. Thus at some point when these creeping changes have accumulated sufficiently to justify a higher pay level, an employee's position should be re-described and re-evaluated. If the position does fall into a higher pay grade and the employee is effectually performing these duties, he should be eligible for a promotional increase. Such raises are not always precisely labeled as promotional, however. Frequently companies will handle these promotions in the normal salary planning process, recognizing that the higher pay level warrants a larger increase, but not identifying which part of the increase is merit and which part promotion.

Upgrading

Upgrading occurs when a given position is re-evaluated into a higher pay level. A job may be upgraded because the scope of assigned duties and responsibilities has increased, although additional responsibilities have not been assigned. Or upgrading may just reflect new thinking or changed thinking on the part of the evaluators.

Some companies handle upgradings exactly like promotions, reasoning that upgrading does indeed reflect increased levels of responsibility regardless of the causes. Other companies establish the higher pay classification but permit no pay action at the time of the upgrading. This course is logical, for instance, when the scope of duties in the future might equally well decline as increase. It also avoids the possibility that re-evaluation might be imprudent and later regretted. Companies which follow this approach do, of course, consider the higher pay grade in determining future merit increases, so that upgrading does enhance income opportunities in the long run.

Downgrading

The same circumstances that would result in upgrading could conceivably lead to downgrading. It is seldom that a company reduces the rate of pay of an individual when a position is downgraded, because the changed classification in no way reflects on his performance. Almost invariably company practice is to establish the new pay classification, so that the employee's income opportunities in the future are diminished. Downgradings involve manpower planning and placement problems, because if the employees were performing properly at the higher-rated job, they are now being underused.

Demotions

Demotion, the opposite of promotion, means that an employee is moved to a lower-rated job. A demotion may occur because the employee's job has been eliminated or substantially changed and there are no jobs available at his current pay level. Or a person may be demoted to a lower-level job because he has failed to perform properly.

Demotions involve broad personnel questions as well as compensation questions. Those reduced in job levels without prejudice should logically be "selected" for demotion. Demotions, like downgradings, also involve manpower planning and placement questions. Company pay practices with respect to employees demoted without prejudice vary greatly. Some continue their former rate of pay, but this may create inequities if demoted employees receive more money than others who may be performing as well, or even better, in the lower-level job. Other companies follow the practice of reducing the employee's pay so that it is in the same relative band position in the new lower pay grade as it was in the former pay grade.

If the demotion is because of unsatisfactory performance, a different situation exists. Normally, disciplinary demotions do call for cutting the employee's pay so that it fits the classification of the new position. This may be done in one reduction, or if it causes undue hardship, over a period of time. In disciplinary cases, many companies follow the practice of discharging the employee rather than demoting him, on the grounds that in the long run, discharge is in his best interest as well as the company's.

Re-evaluation and Inequity Increases

Re-evaluation increases generally refer to special adjustments permitted for recently hired or promoted employees in recognition of demonstrated abilities and aptitudes far beyond those originally assessed when the employee was placed in the job. Such increases have the virtue of correcting past mistakes. Their existence, however, may encourage ultraconservatism in hiring rates or even loose employment screening procedures.

"Inequity increase" is generally a label attached to one that cannot be classified elsewhere. Where used, the term tends to reflect the fact that practical considerations such as market competition, internal pay relationships, and other factors are being considered in setting the employee's pay. The same objective can be achieved without such a label, however, if the merit increase program is broad enough to allow supervisors to review all pertinent factors to reach pay increase decisions.

Red-Circle Situations

Red-circle situations refer to cases where the employee's pay is above the maximum of the pay range in which his position is classified. There is seldom any question of reducing pay in red-circle situations; rather, the problem is whether to withhold further increases.

Good business practice dictates that in such cases the employee's pay will be "frozen," and he will not be eligible for increase until the structure has been adjusted upward to the point where his pay is within range. This is desirable for three reasons. First, unless pay-range maximums are enforced, they are meaningless. Second, in red-circle situations the employee is being paid more than an outstanding rate for his performance. There is already an inequity, since he receives more money than others within range who are doing outstanding work. Third, unless the company has unlimited resources, any additional amount granted to red-circle employees must be made at the expense of others who are paid less for the same or even better performance.

Sometimes supervisors are too apologetic toward employees who cannot be given additional merit increases because they receive red-circle rates or are at the top of their range. The fact is that if the company's pay structures are properly set, these employees are receiving outstanding pay. One large firm in the glass industry takes a positive approach to such situations. On the company bulletin board the employees who are at the maximum of their range are listed and identified as people who have demonstrated superior performance and have been rewarded with outstanding pay.

Some companies allow modest and infrequent increases in red-circle situations, so that the structure catches up more gradually to the incumbent's pay. Special types of control are necessary when such a practice is followed.

Gold-Circle Situations

A gold circle situation is a case where the employee's pay is over the maximum of his evaluated pay level, but where he should be exempted from red-circle ground rules. Basically, there are two gold-circle situations. In the first one, the incumbent is in a training position, and the work he is performing does not reflect his capabilities or the level of duties he is qualified for. The second case is where the incumbent deserves a promotion to a significantly higher level, but for the time being no opening is available. In both cases, the usual practice is to exempt these individuals from the salary administration program until such time as they can take their proper place in it.

Green-Circle Situations

This label applies to situations where an employee's pay is below the minimum of his job classification. In theory, all employees should be raised to the minimum of their range as a matter of simple equity. However, where there are large numbers of green-circle cases, either because of a job re-evaluation project or some major organizational change, there are practical drawbacks to raising everyone immediately to the minimum. For one thing, significant costs may be involved. For another, new inequities may be created between the newly raised employees and those who were already at the minimum of the range. Furthermore, there is always the danger that either a position is overclassified or the employee in it is underqualified. For these reasons, careful review and phasing-in periods are frequently appropriate.

Silver-Circle Situations

Some companies grant very long service employees pay increases even when they are not justified on the basis of performance. These are the situations which are sometimes labeled silver-circle increases.

The advantages and disadvantages of length-of-service increases have already been reviewed. Some companies, however, regard these increases as being in the same category as the 25-year service pin. Where such increases are clearly for very long service, are identified as extra payments solely for service, and are separately budgeted, they can be of some value. It goes without saying that they should not be granted at the expense of other increases earned by performance improvement.

TOP MANAGEMENT CONTROL

In addition to following laws and ground rules established to *guide* managerial decisions, top management must establish controls to make sure that the pay program achieves its objectives. Adequate management control represents the difference between delegation of responsibility and abdication of responsibility. There are four types of controls that are available to top management in wage and salary administration: budgetary controls, statistical controls, control by approval, and control by influence.

Budgetary Controls

Experience indicates that one of the truly essential elements of successful salary administration is an effective budgetary system. Budgets serve primarily as a control, but they are also necessary for effective delegation of salary actions to the first level of supervision.

There are actually two types of budgets—payroll and merit. Payroll budgets involve total dollars of payroll allocated to various operating units. These gross figures include considerations of turnover, pay increases of all types, and, most important of all, the numbers of persons in each unit. Such budgets are valuable in financial forecasting, cash management, and other accounting controls. They do not really serve the purpose of controlling the equitable distribution of pay-increase dollars.

A merit budget, on the other hand, specifies the amount allocated for merit increases to each division, department, section, and unit of the company. It tells the supervisors how much they may spend and also how much they should spend.

One method of preparing merit increase budgets is illustrated in Exhibit 18. To determine a control curve, we need only two points. One is fixed in the sense that if maximums of pay ranges are to be enforced, then, when the average band position is 100 percent, the merit increase budget should be zero. To determine the second point, we need both a calculation and a management decision. The calculation is simply the statistical determination of average band position for the overall operation. The decision involves the determination on the vertical axis of

EXHIBIT 18
MERIT BUDGET CONTROL CURVES

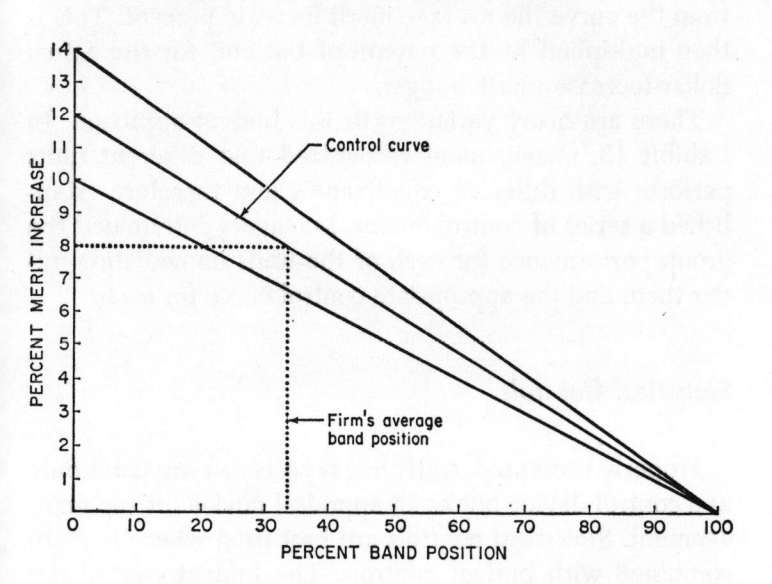

[Graph: Percent Merit Increase (y-axis, 0–14) vs. Percent Band Position (x-axis, 0–100). Three control curves converge at 100. Dashed lines indicate Firm's average band position at ~33% intersecting control curve at 8%.]

the point marked as X in the exhibit. This percent should equal the average merit increase which management feels appropriate for the year. It should be selected on the basis of such factors as the following:

- Competitiveness of company pay levels in the labor markets.
- Information on other merit-increase budgets and amounts granted by competitors in the labor market.
- Financial ability to pay.
- Cost-of-living trend since the last adjustment of the salary structure.
- Company compensation policies.
- Increases in productivity in the work group.

Once established, the X amount and the average band position set a second point on the graph, and a control curve can be drawn. Management can use this curve to determine the appropriate budget for every unit simply by calculating the band position for the unit and reading from the curve the average merit increase percent. This is then multiplied by the payroll of the unit for the actual dollar-increase merit budget.

There are many variations of this budget approach. In Exhibit 18, management recognized that different units perform with different effectiveness and therefore established a series of control curves. Managers determined the group performance for each of the units immediately under them and the appropriate control curve for each.

Statistical Controls

Properly presented, statistical reports can serve not only as a control device but as an appraisal device for top management. Statistical controls are best used when they are combined with budget controls. The budget control devices guide before the fact; the statistical devices report after the fact.

The salary planning sheets described in Chapter IV are themselves a method of statistical control. A second basic type of statistical report merely tabulates the amount expended for merit increases and other increases in each unit against the amount budgeted. Other useful information includes data on: the number of positions which have been re-evaluated and the results of re-evaluation; the dispersion of job classifications by organizational units and analysis of significant trends in dispersion patterns; dispersion in merit pay increases; reporting of money expended by units for increases other than merit increases; and grievances with respect to pay classifications or pay changes.

If properly geared to the business, these reports can tell

management a great deal about how well salary administration programs are operating. They can also give valuable insight into the effectiveness of supervision.

Control by Approval

Approval requirements, the most traditional method of management control, provide management with the opportunity of reviewing each pay action. They undoubtedly have some control value and some value in keeping higher-level management informed about people as well as pay actions.

Approval requirements alone, however, have been proved inadequate as a control device. Unless a manager is in a position to know the facts surrounding each individual pay change, it is difficult for him to approve, disapprove, or modify. Only immediate supervisors can be adequately informed about such crucial questions as employee performance, the possibility of quitting, relationships within a group, or the potential of individual employees. Thus, in the reviewing process, the higher-level supervisor should concentrate upon assuring himself that all relevant factors have been considered and that the immediate supervisor has done a thoughtful job in reaching decisions.

Frequently, approval requirements have become obstacle courses. Just how many approvals should be obtained depends upon company organization and the type of pay program in effect. It is hard to believe, however, that there is any real need for, or any genuine value in, having on a pay change slip more than the signature of the immediate supervisor, one personnel representative, and the next two higher levels of line management.

As a matter of procedure, it is wise to review proposed

pay changes with the personnel representative before submitting them for higher-level line management approval. In this way the reviewing supervisor can be sure that the immediate supervisor has complied with any policies and ground rules and that the action is consistent with company practices. This review also makes it possible for the personnel specialist to play the constructive role of counselor and technical adviser rather than that of an instrument of control.

Control by Influence

An effective though indirect method of control is to take steps which will help managers make sound pay decisions in the first place. To achieve this, the company will ideally—

1. Provide managers with the information they need in order to reach proper decisions.
2. Develop and install sound compensation techniques (for example, job evaluation).
3. Provide managers with sensible compensation policies supplemented by constructive and logical ground rules.
4. Communicate these policies and ground rules to the supervisors.
5. Train managers in the basic thinking and techniques of sound salary practices.
6. Give managers the time to do a careful job in making pay decisions.
7. Make managers truly accountable for their pay decisions.

This thinking suggests that the company should train subordinate managers to make logical and equitable pay decisions rather than take the punitive approach of correcting mistakes after they are made. Such a constructive policy considers individual review, not as a means of reversing the supervisor's decisions but as an opportunity to train him in making better decisions.

Another type of constructive action involves the positive use of a personnel specialist. Instead of exercising a strictly control function, which tends to make review a rigid and inflexible process calculated mainly to assure the purity of the techniques and ground rules, the personnel specialist could work constructively with the managers, helping them solve compensation problems, making concrete suggestions in the area of salary administration and related subjects, and in general assisting them to increase the effectiveness of their operations. This approach not only results in better compensation decisions but contributes to building management and preserving staff.

SPECIAL ADMINISTRATIVE CONSIDERATIONS

The wide variety of special considerations and administrative matters which are inherent in a wage and salary program lie primarily in the realm of top management and the personnel specialist. However, since the individual supervisor should at least be cognizant of them, a few of these matters are outlined here with brief comments.

Interface Problems

Most companies have more than one group of employees. For example, there may be production workers, skilled plant workers, office employees, draftsmen and technicians, supervisory, administrative, and technical personnel, sales personnel, professional employees, managers, and executives. Some companies have as few as two or three of these groups; others have as many as eight. To some degree there are separate salary administration practices and techniques applied to each. Frequently, the pay of different groups overlaps.

These differences may lead to interface problems. For instance, if a different merit budget, rate of progress, or salary structure is applied to production employees from that applied to office employees, pay relationships between the groups may become distorted. This not only may create inequities but may impede the transfer of employees.

Somewhat different pay practices are generally applied to different groups of employees. Typically, for instance, office workers tend to get weekly pay, rather than the hourly pay of production workers, and more flexibility in terms of timekeeping and hours of work. In each of the company's groups there are usually some unique pay practices, and these should be related to the unique nature of the duties performed by the groups. It is important for the supervisor to know which differences do exist and what the reasons for them are; otherwise he may not be able to administer the differences or explain them.

Career Compensations

Some of the questions which supervisors face in wage and salary administration involve career patterns of income improvement for employees. Exhibit 19 shows three common patterns. Curve A illustrates the typical pattern of income improvement for a given job or a progressive family of jobs (such as mechanical engineer I, II, III, and so on). Note that income improves rapidly when the employee first comes on the job and that the rate of improve-

EXHIBIT 19
Hypothetical Career Compensation Curve

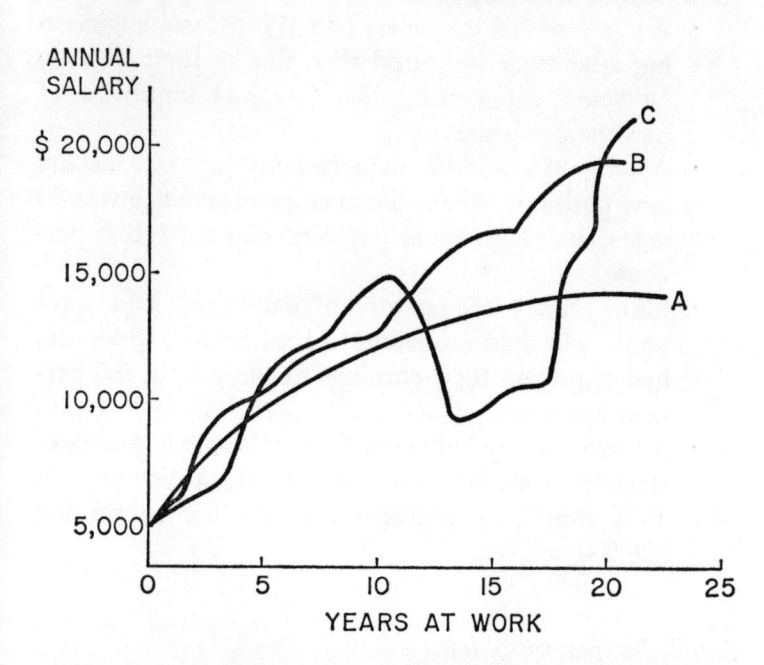

ment gradually slows down until it reaches a point where further increases are very modest. Most employees, however, do not spend their entire careers on one job or even one family of jobs. Their career curves then resemble curve B, which is like a series of A curves joined together. Alternatively, the income curve of an individual may vary greatly and be quite irregular. Frequently, for instance, it will show a distinct upward thrust sometime between the ages of 30 and 40. Or a person's income curve may actually decline a period, as shown in the curve C.

Information not only on the shape of these career curves but also on the amount of overall improvement could be valuable to management in establishing wage and salary programs. Unfortunately, little concrete data are available in these areas. The few studies which have been made show some interesting facts:

- A study of 200 engineers in a West Coast engineering laboratory indicated that, during their average 14 years' experience, their pay had improved 11 percent per year.
- Among 374 middle management persons seeking new positions, where the average experience was 20 years, average annual pay had improved 13.5 percent.
- More than 1,000 nonexempt employees in a company, who had an average of 14 years' experience, had improved their earnings at the rate of 6.5 percent per year.
- A further study indicated that high school graduates starting at an average salary of $3,500 per year in 1965 would, by retirement at age 65, be earning $25,000 per year.

Small-Company Problems

The basic problem which is faced by small companies in connection with wage and salary administration is that many of the techniques described here are costly and there are not enough people covered by the program to make many of them valid. The principles discussed in this book still apply but simpler techniques might well be more appropriate. For instance, even though managers anywhere must have the requisite knowledge of job duties and values, they can acquire it from very brief position descriptions instead of elaborate formats and procedures. And simple ranking techniques will do the evaluation job satisfactorily for the smaller organization.

Moreover, while this smaller company may have the disadvantage of not being able to utilize sophisticated techniques, it has many advantages. One of the most important is the greater familiarity with jobs and people possessed by management. Another is the greater consistency gained when only one or a few persons administer the pay program. Probably the greatest advantage of all is management's ability to react quickly to situations and to explain on a person-to-person basis the decisions which are made.

Problems of Large Companies

Problems common to all large companies are those of communication, training, consistency, and coordination. Many large companies also face the basic problem of relating compensation decisions and policy to the basic goals and business philosophy of the enterprise. While this is difficult, the solution usually begins with top management's identifying and communicating the goals and essential thinking of the company and ends with supervisors' listening.

A second type of problem common to many large companies involves geographic differences in pay levels. Fundamentally, these differences are caused, not by differences in cost of living, but rather by differences in the composition of the industry in different localities. Since these differences do exist and are very real, large companies frequently relate pay and pay structure to community pay levels. Otherwise, employees in some areas would be relatively underpaid, or else employees in most areas would be relatively overpaid.

A third problem faced by most large companies involves

the decision-making authority to be vested at the corporate, division, and location levels. Generally speaking, the answer to this question must reflect the organization of the line. For instance, if the company is highly decentralized in its line decision making, then most fundamental decisions with respect to salary administration must be made at the location. The key to working through this problem in large companies is usually to develop a framework for decision making. This involves a simple identification of activities, methods, or programs and the establishment for each of a decision-making center.

General Increases

Many companies grant general increases—that is, increases which go to everyone—for at least some groups of employees. Usually the reason for such an approach is that there are overall economic factors which apply equally to every employee regardless of his length of service or performance. To the degree that this is true, there is indeed equity in giving everyone the same increase.

Sometimes these increases are tied to the cost of living. Cost-of-living considerations can, however, be applied to groups of employees only where there are cost of living measures available. Thus they can logically be applied only to factory workers or those at equivalent income levels, for the only available measure of cost-of-living changes is the Bureau of Labor Statistics' consumer's price index, which is related to the market basket of a factory worker with a family of four.

When general increases are tied in with a merit increase program, it is extremely important for managers to recognize frankly that some part of an employee's increase really represents a general increase. Nothing makes an employee more cynical than to see a factory worker, for example, receive a 4 percent increase and then to get an increase of his own, supposedly for merit, which also amounts to 4 percent. To avoid this, some companies have separated merit increases and general increases. Others, which have integrated the two, have found it wise to explain to employees frankly that part of the increase is really a general increase. Employees who are doing as well in their work as they were previously tend to get the general increase automatically. The balance of any increase represents an improvement in pay and can be explained on the basis of improved performance or other considerations.

Keeping the Program Up to Date

Supervisors sometimes feel that the problems of pay administration have been solved once a formal salary administration program is installed. Actually, of course, unless a program is kept up to date and adapted to changing circumstances, the company will very shortly have no program at all.

To keep the program up to date technically means: (1) keeping descriptions up to date so that at all times the existing position descriptions accurately reflect duties assigned; (2) keeping evaluation judgments up to date so that evaluations represent management's best thinking, guided by the evaluation program as to the relative worth of all positions; (3) keeping the pay structure up to date so that it is indeed reasonable and competitive.

Such technical matters can be achieved very simply. The more difficult problem is to keep the program up to date substantively. Essentially, this requires that supervisors use the system which is in effect and use it with good judgment, for the key to the success of any good technique is sound management practice.

Cost of Wage and Salary Administration

The cost of wage and salary administration varies substantially. A true cost estimate must include some measure of supervisor time and employee time, as well as the expense of staff work and outside consulting services. The total cost depends mostly upon the level of the jobs covered and the nature of the program. The following guides might apply to a program covering supervisory, administrative, and technical persons: (1) cost of installing the program—$50 to $100 per employee; (2) cost of administering an already established program—one-quarter to one-half of 1 percent of the payroll.

The cost will be substantially higher for programs covering management and professional employees and somewhat lower for programs covering production or office employees. In any case, of course, they are considerable. Because of the size of the investment, the program should certainly contribute significantly to the solution of company pay problems and the achievement of company goals.

CHAPTER VI

WAGE INCENTIVE PLANS

Under certain conditions employees are rewarded for their individual contribution by incentive payments instead of by extra compensation granted under a merit rating plan. This chapter will outline incentive plans for plant workers, and the following chapters will describe incentive plans for salesmen, professional employees, and managers.

Logic of Wage Incentive Plans

Wage incentive plans and merit rating plans have many common characteristics. In both systems, job rates are determined through job evaluation. In both, individual employees are paid a premium which is geared in some manner to individual performance above minimum requirements.

The logic of these individual premium payments is based upon the fact that people vary in almost every possible respect: in strength, vitality, ability, and desire to produce on the job. Because of these differences, a group of employees—all qualified to do a given job—can perform at widely divergent speeds. The assumption of both merit rating and incentive plans is that if the company gears extra pay to extra work, each employee will tend to produce to the maximum of his individual ability.

Incentive plans attempt to motivate employees to perform above the standard by creating a direct relationship between physical units produced and employee compensation. A standard is first established that specifies how many units of output are expected in return for the job rate. In theory, this calls for an equal effort from all employees. Any production above this minimum is assumed to be the result of greater effort, and the employee is given additional pay for it in direct proportion to the extra amount he produces. Since the incentive approach assumes that the output can be physically counted, it is applicable primarily to production jobs.

Basically, this wage incentive approach represents a unique concept of worker payment. Other systems pay the employee for the time he is on the job, and it is the task of management to utilize that time effectively. Under the incentive system, the employee's pay is geared primarily to the number of units he produces regardless of how much time is required.

Types of Incentive Plans

Over the years, individual companies have developed a bewildering array of incentive plans; some of these are quite direct and simple to understand, while others are extremely complex and technical. The most widely used are the piecework plan, the Taylor differential piece-rate plan, the Halsey gain-share plan, the standard-hour plan, and the various point incentive and group incentive systems. There are, of course, innumerable variations and combinations of these.

The piecework plan. As the name suggests, under this plan the employee's earnings are directly related to the number of units he produces; he receives a fixed price or wage for each unit he turns out. The piecework plan, which was the first incentive system to be developed, is one of the most popular in industry. It has the advantage of establishing a direct relationship between what a worker produces and what he earns.

Taylor differential piece-rate plan. This system, originally developed by Frederick W. Taylor, is the same as the piecework approach except that it has two rates. The higher rate is paid when the worker equals or betters the standard established for each job; the lower is paid when output is less than standard. This arrangement provides the workers with an incentive to produce at least the standard.

Halsey gain-share plan. A standard time is established for each task, and the employee receives a base rate of pay for production completed within the time. However, if he finishes the task in less than the time allotted, he receives a bonus which is generally equal to about half the saving in time. The bonus earnings are added to the base earnings, and an earned rate is calculated for the purpose of computing overtime hours.

Standard-hour plan. This system is similar to the Halsey plan except that employees receive a 100 percent premium. In other words, an employee's bonus is equal to 100 percent of the savings effected by his greater productivity.

Point incentive wage systems. Under these systems, the standard for each operation is first determined, including allowances for rest or relaxation. The standards are translated into point values, and incentive pay is then geared to the employee's ability to perform in less than standard time. Since all jobs are measured in points, it is possible to make simple comparisons of performance on jobs that have dissimilar work cycles.

Group incentive systems. The various techniques described above have also been applied on a group basis in situations where a group of employees works as a team. In such cases, it is not practical to apply incentives individually; they are based upon the output of the group as a whole, with each member sharing proportionately in the bonus.

Methods of Determining Work Standards

Selecting the appropriate incentive plan for a given company, and deciding which method to use in setting standards are usually the tasks of the industrial engineering specialist. All incentive pay programs require a predetermined standard, and the extent to which they attain the basic objective of gearing pay directly to production depends on the standard's accuracy.

Standards may be established in three different ways. The simplest is to base them upon past performance—to analyze production records and take some percentage of past work attainment as the standard for the future. This approach is, of course, extremely hazardous. Records reflect only what qualified workers have done, not what they could possibly do. Experience has shown that past performance may represent as little as 30 or 40 percent of a reasonable standard of work. This is particularly true if methods have been loose, supervision has been lax, or scheduling and production planning faulty.

Because of the obvious pitfalls of basing standards strictly on past performance, most plans use at least some form of time study, in which a trained industrial engineer actually observes the operation and records the time necessary to accomplish it. He also judges the percentage of efficiency of the worker he is observing so that this factor can be taken into consideration. The accuracy of time and motion studies depends upon how closely the engineer observes the job and how well he estimates the worker's efficiency.

A third and still more refined method of determining work standards is to apply time values that have already been established for every conceivable type of worker motion. These values are based on years of observation and study in many different production situations. In using them to set standards, it is not even necessary to estimate the worker's efficiency; this has already been built into the standard time values. The industrial engineer needs only to observe and record each motion and attach the standard time value to it. The standard for that particular task is then set after making proper allowances for rest and down time. This method not only eliminates a large area of variability due to individual judgment, but also permits more careful study of the job.

Economics of Wage Incentive Systems

While the economics of wage incentive plans varies somewhat depending upon the type of plan used, it does have a basic impact on earnings and costs. This is illustrated in Exhibit 20. Up to the point of standard production under most plans, employees are guaranteed a fixed hourly rate, which averages $2.40 per hour in the exhibit. After the standard is exceeded, the average hourly earnings increase in direct relationship to increased output. In Exhibit 20, the increase is from $2.40 to a maximum of $3.00. At the same time, the unit costs, which are a combination of the direct costs of labor and material and the fixed overhead costs, drop rapidly as employees work toward standard production, and they continue to decrease as employees pass standard. This is because the increase in direct costs caused by increasing hourly rates is more

EXHIBIT 20
Economics of Wage Incentive Plans

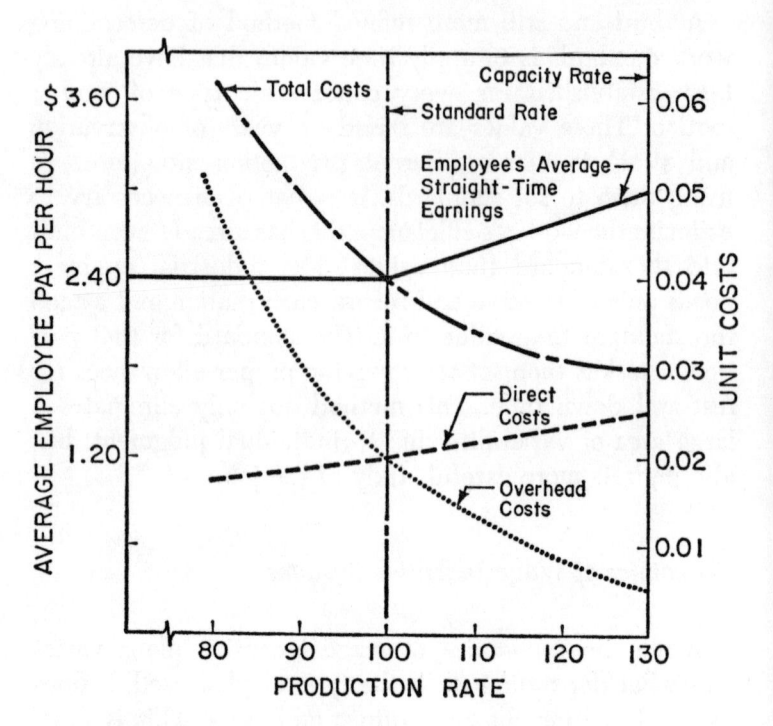

than offset by the drop in fixed overhead costs. As a result, by motivating employees to produce more on the job, companies can accomplish the double objective of increasing employee earnings and reducing unit costs.

It is the worst sort of oversimplification, however, to assume that the mere establishment of an incentive plan can motivate workers to higher output, reduce unit costs, and result in both higher employee earnings and greater company profits. In order to obtain a more realistic outlook on the impact of an incentive plan on a business operation, managers must also consider such questions as these: How much does money motivate employees? What is the effect of higher output on costs? What additional factors influence both output and cost, and what effect does an incentive plan have on them? What other considerations lead a company to establish an incentive plan?

Money and motivation. Higher earnings are certainly one of the means of motivating workers—perhaps the principal means in most situations. However, employee effectiveness is also influenced by such things as job security, fringe benefits, general working conditions, safety conditions, and the general management "climate."

In certain circumstances, establishment of an incentive system not only has failed to increase production, but has caused an actual reduction in employee productivity. For instance, one company which moved into a low-wage area in the South found that substantial increases in pay through incentive systems merely resulted in higher absenteeism. Once they had earned what they considered necessary or desirable, employees would take time off rather than work additional hours for more money. In other cases, incentive plans have seemed to cause employees to restrict output, bargain for lower work standards, and generally try to get higher pay without increased effort.

Output and cost. It would also be erroneous to suppose that increased output automatically leads to a reduction in unit costs. For one thing, wage incentive systems themselves frequently involve extra costs, including the cost of grievances resulting from questions of work standards and incentive rates, the cost of maintaining the larger industrial engineering department that is required, and the administrative costs associated with an incentive plan.

Operating managers should recognize that employee effort on the job is only one factor influencing output and cost. Greater employee productivity and lower unit costs can be obtained in several other ways:

1. Full utilization of plant capacity.
2. Simplification and standardization of products and their components.
3. More effective utilization of materials, supplies, and the various services that go into production; or the use of less costly materials and supplies and the elimination of services that may actually not be necessary.
4. Improved methods and procedures of work. Included, of course, are more efficient machinery, jigs, fixtures, and other equipment; more efficient layouts; better work areas; better planning and scheduling; more effective machine loading; and so on.
5. Improvement of workers' effectiveness through the development of skills, assistance in planning the work, nonmonetary incentives, and better utilization of their time.

Other objectives of incentive plans. Managers should also recognize that while increased employee earnings and lower unit costs may be the primary reason for establishing incentive plans, there may be other important objectives too. For instance, some companies have installed incentive plans in part because they contribute flexibility to operations which are subject to significant fluctuation. When business is brisk, greater effort on the job may meet the extra production requirements. When business slows down, the incentive plan helps to prevent layoffs. Other companies have established incentive plans because they result in greater use of equipment and facilities and thereby conserve capital.

Elements of a Sound Wage Incentive System

Experience with 211 types of plans has shown that certain requirements must be met.

- The program must be technically sound.
- The standards established must be guaranteed to employees.
- Reasonable incentive earnings must be maintained.
- Basic work methods must be enforced.
- A balance in total pay relationships must be preserved.
- The program, including work standards, must be kept up to date as methods, materials, and equipment change.
- The program must contribute to higher productivity and to the long-range growth and success of the company.

Technical soundness. First, it is essential that the company have some sound and reasonably objective means of setting work standards. Otherwise, increased worker effort may not be the primary cause of increased production. It is also important that workers be able to understand the foundation upon which their incentive earnings are based. Preferably, the plan should be so simple that workers, knowing the amount they produce each day or each hour, can determine for themselves what their incentive earnings should be. The incentive formula not only should be understandable but also should establish some direct relationship between the earnings of the employee and the quantity and quality of his output. Finally, incentive earnings should be sufficiently generous to convince workers that they are being adequately paid for their extra effort.

Guaranteed standards. If there is one single factor that has caused both employees and trade unions to oppose the application of these plans, it is the history of rate cutting which has occurred throughout industry where incentive plans have been in effect. Certainly, when a worker has increased his earnings because of his own application or ingenuity on the job, he will resist any cut in the rate. Not only has rate cutting resulted in the more direct and obvious retaliation of employees who quit or strike, but it has also led to such practices as collusion to withhold work or to peg the output on the job.

The guaranteeing of work standards does not mean, of course, that they can never be changed. It means only that management promises not to change the work standards unless there is a genuine change in methods, materials, or equipment on the job. When the job does change, a new standard should be set.

Reasonable incentive earnings. If standards are so high that only a few workers can possibly earn premium pay, then there is not much actual incentive in the incentive program. With reasonable effort, most workers should be able to attain some incentive earnings. In addition, the incentive formula should contain special provisions for breakdown in equipment, material trouble, and other delays or interruptions in work. On the other hand, work standards and controls should not be so loose that incentive earnings constitute a disproportionate share of total earnings. Average premiums of 15 to 25 percent are generally considered proper. Finally, incentive earnings should not become a substitute for general increases in base pay. Certainly the incentive system will soon get into trouble if the company expects that incentive pay will eliminate the employee's desire for general increases based upon trends in wages and the cost of living.

Enforcement of work methods. Under a sound incentive plan, the company should engineer each task to determine the best method, set standards based upon that best method, and require workers to follow it. This assumes that it is management's responsibility to improve methods, equipment, and material, while it is the worker's responsibility to apply himself reasonably to the job, following the methods that have been established. Unless this procedure is adopted, the company may find itself in a position where employees have improved the methods so much that they are either earning an unreasonable amount of incentive pay or attaining high incentive pay with minimum effort.

Balance in total pay relationships. The whole question of consistent standards and uniform application has an important bearing upon gross pay relationships within the company. Where standards are not consistently set on all jobs, it becomes possible for workers in some jobs to attain higher incentive earnings without any additional effort. By the same token, where standards are not enforced, some employees will work harder to improve methods than others. In either case, gross earnings on different jobs can vary widely, and workers on jobs with relatively low base rates can earn considerably more than highly skilled workers.

Contribution to successful operations. There is, finally, the broad requirement that the incentive plan must contribute to the long-range success and growth of the business. Otherwise the investment necessary to establish and administer the plan cannot be justified. This requirement has many ramifications.

For example, personnel policies must be established which take into account the worker's skill, his versatility, his length of service, and any other attributes which may be important to the company in the long run. In addition, the company must adopt procedures and controls to insure that greater quantity of production is not obtained at the cost of poorer quality. Again, the entire wage incentive program must be acceptable to union representatives; otherwise the company may become embroiled in continuous collective bargaining over standards, work methods, and incentive earnings. Then, too, the incentive plan should not seriously impede the flexibility that the company must have in assigning work and in transferring employees. Finally, establishment of an incentive plan should not lead to the deterioration of management practices.

Administration of the Plan

Just how well managers meet their responsibilities under the wage incentive program is every bit as important to its success as the technical aspects of the plan. Managers, particularly first-line supervisors, have responsibilities in the areas of establishing and enforcing work methods; establishing and reviewing work standards; training employees to follow correct methods; supervising work flow, materials, equipment, and the administrative aspects of incentive plans; and, handling communications regarding incentives, including questions and complaints.

Establishing work methods not only is important to the success of the incentive program but also constitutes a basic determinant of shop efficiency. A fundamental management responsibility, it involves the choice of the proper equipment, layout, process, and materials, as well as stipulation of the proper motions which the workers should make. Theoretically, there is an ideal method for any one job, and it is this method which management should seek to discover.

Certainly this responsibility should not be delegated to workers. Employees may, largely through trial and error, devise more efficient motions and techniques, but they are hardly in a position to determine equipment, flow, materials, and so forth. In fact, their innovations may have adverse effects on equipment life, work flow, product quality, or safety practices. (This is not to say that workers cannot *participate* in developing efficient methods, either formally through a suggestion system or informally by working with industrial engineers.)

Just as managers must play an active role in determining proper work methods, so they should have some control over the standards which are set on these methods. Although industrial engineers may actually study the job and establish the standards, the manager concerned must at least review them, since he is held accountable for costs and employee relations. If standards are too loose, costs will be out of line; if they are too tight, trouble with employees or unions is inevitable.

After both methods and standards are set, it is the duty of the manager to make sure that employees observe them. First of all, this involves training workers on the job, particularly if they are expected to follow company-determined work standards. Job training frequently requires more than merely telling the employee what to do; the supervisor may have to show him how to do it, observe him doing it, and tell him when he is doing it improperly. The quality of job training influences not only how much workers produce but also how quickly they learn the job.

Besides skillful training, enforcement of standards and methods requires effective daily supervision, which includes assignment of duties, discipline, and reward. People vary in their aptitude for different types of work—to the point where an employee who makes 30 percent more in incentive pay on one job may have difficulty attaining standard pay on another. Proper assignment of workers to the jobs for which they are best suited can contribute substantially to worker achievement.

In addition to proper assignment plus proper training, however, managers must motivate workers on the job. Such motivation is an indefinable activity. Certainly, it involves follow-up by the supervisor, so that workers not only know what is expected of them but are sure that the boss knows what they accomplish. The manager who is successful in motivating his employees also has a sensitivity to work problems and to the worker as an individual, an ability to identify problems which interfere with employee efficiency, and a certain social grace which defies description because it is so highly individualized.

Both reward and discipline play a role in assuring proper worker attainment of work standards. Incentive plans themselves are designed to give material reward automatically. In addition, greater recognition, more rapid promotion, preferential treatment in job assignments, and other personnel devices may be utilized to reward the particularly effective worker and provide extra incentive pay for him.

For those who do not attain reasonable standards of production, some form of discipline is necessary. The supervisor would be unfair to these employees who do perform effectively, as well as to the company and himself, if he did not use discipline when necessary. Ideally, discipline is proportioned to the offense, geared to correction and preventing abuses rather than to mere punishment, and applied only after careful investigation of the facts and surrounding circumstances.

Finally, the manager of each operating department plays a key role in explaining the incentive program to employees. Unless they believe the plan to be fair, and believe that extra effort on their part will bring about commensurate increases in their earnings, it is not likely to motivate them to substantially greater production. In addition, workers will inevitably have questions and complaints, and it will be largely up to the supervisor to handle and answer them. Many grievances concern the fairness of the standard in the first place. It is usually not enough for the supervisor to call on the industrial engineer who established the standard to recheck it for accuracy. The manager must himself review it and assure himself of its accuracy; he should not simply act as the spokesman for another's judgment.

WAGE INCENTIVE PLANS

Even this brief summary of the supervisor's responsibilities under wage incentive programs indicates that those who see these plans as being largely self-supervisory are badly mistaken. The manager's responsibilities under incentive pay and day-work pay plans may differ somewhat in areas of emphasis, but they are equally great for both programs.

CHAPTER VII

SALESMEN'S COMPENSATION

IN ALL BUSINESSES, DISTRIBUTION IS A KEY PART OF COMpany operations, and the effectiveness of distribution usually depends in large part on the field sales force. A major portion of sales expense is personnel. Thus, from the viewpoint of both effectiveness and cost, the issues concerning salesmen's compensation are vitally important to management.

The Sales Job: A Definition

There may have been a time when sales jobs were easy to identify and simple to define, but in most enterprises today they are not. Typically, sales personnel perform at least some nonsales work, and many nonsales personnel are in some way related to the selling activity.

In a broader sense, everyone who affects the quality of the product, the service rendered, the image of the company, or relationships with customers is a "salesman." Many persons who are not considered salesmen devote their entire time to professional, technical, or administrative work supporting the sales effort. Some actually have direct selling responsibility even though their primary job may be professional or managerial. For instance, a lawyer who performs legal work for clients is certainly expected to be alert to opportunities for additional legal assignments.

None of these persons, however, would be defined as a salesman for the purpose of personnel administration or compensation. Strictly speaking, a salesman works with buyers to procure orders. He spends the bulk of his time doing this, and it constitutes the main activity for which he is paid.

Salesmen's Duties

Most sales positions involve a variety of duties which might include some of the following.

Soliciting orders. Certainly, every sales job entails the actual solicitation of orders. To understand the job, however, it is also necessary to know the specific product line for which the salesman is responsible; the number of customers and who they are; the total sales volume and the volume by line; the number of units, sales transactions and buying decisions; the number of times that each customer will probably be visited; and what takes place during the visit.

Servicing orders. Many sales jobs have important servicing responsibilities. In fact, it is sometimes difficult to distinguish between a solicitation call and a servicing call.

Prospecting. This involves ferreting out new potential users of the company's goods or services.

"Missionary" work. The salesman may be expected to undertake direct promotion or merchandising, train customer personnel in use of products or services, or give technical advice and administrative assistance.

Accumulating information. Inherent in every sales job is some requirement for the accumulation of information

—for example, information about the customer, persons within the customer's organization, and potential customers in the district. The salesman may also send information to headquarters about markets, customers' requirements, forecasts, competitors' products, and new possibilities. Finally, he must receive information from headquarters pertaining to policies, products, methods, service available, and so on.

Management decisions. Many salesmen who spend the majority of their time in direct selling also have management responsibilities—for a few salesmen, for office personnel, or for storage facilities. In addition, salesmen sometimes make management decisions involving credit, pricing, and product adaptation or modification.

Nonsales work. All salesmen have some administrative responsibility, which includes making reports and keeping records of some sort.

Knowledge of a particular sales job also requires an understanding of the marketing operations of the company—including the markets themselves, the competition, alternative or substitute products, distributive systems, the nature of the demand for the product, the nature of the sales transaction, the degree of product differentiation, and the sophistication of the buyers. Knowledge of the product itself is also essential. For instance, is it a technical or nontechnical product? A product or a system of products? A product or a service? Finally, it is important to know whether the salesman handles the sales transaction independently or works as part of a selling team.

The overwhelming variety in sales jobs is at the heart of the complexities of sales compensation. It results in a great number and diversity of sales compensation plans, as well as frequent changes in the details of sales compensation programs. One study of nine leading companies in an industry, for example, revealed nine different sales compensation plans. It also showed that in a five-year period the nine companies had made significant changes in these plans.

Sales Job Descriptions

Whether or not a company should use job descriptions for salesmen depends primarily on how many sales positions it has, how complex they are, and how much is known about them by the people who make the pay decisions. Various studies indicate that between 50 and 75 percent of companies do use sales job descriptions. As a rule of thumb, a firm which has more than two dozen salesman *positions* (not salesmen) will find position descriptions not only desirable but essential.

The appropriate format for sales job descriptions is frequently different from that for production and office workers. The information needed involves far more than what the salesman does; it also includes such facts as the number of customers, volumes of sales, diversity of products sold, areas covered, and other data of the kind outlined in the previous section. If many elements of the job are similar for all the company's sales positions, however, then the descriptions need only provide the information which discriminates among the various jobs.

Elements of Sales Compensation

Since the basic objectives of salesmen's compensation plans are the same as for any other group of employees, essentially the same elements of compensation administration are applicable. First, as discussed above, it is necessary to understand the jobs involved. Second, there must be a method for determining the relative worth of jobs, with respect both to other sales jobs and to other positions within the organization. Third, the compensation of sales personnel must be related to comparable jobs outside the company. Fourth, outstanding individual achievement must be rewarded. Finally, there are administrative considerations and ground rules, which are not too different from those discussed in Chapter V. In salary administration for sales positions, as for other special groups of jobs, the unique features of a compensation plan lie in its application and methodology, not in its basic requirements.

In the sales compensation area, the primary emphasis is on building as much incentive compensation as possible into the pay program. Since a high percentage of salesmen's pay is often in incentive form, the persons administering the program tend to be highly conscious of such areas as market research, allocation of districts, and assignment of personnel. Frequently, too, personnel and pay administration for salesmen is regarded as an integral part of sales management rather than of personnel management. Finally, geographic dispersions, number of persons involved, and other physical characteristics in the sales force may result in significantly different administrative practices.

Incentive Versus Base Pay

Generally speaking, companies favor some form of incentive compensation for salesmen, not only because of tradition, but because of the importance of sales volume in the success of most businesses, the general dispersion of the sales force, and other elements of sales management. The key to determining the appropriateness of incentive compensation is analysis of sales objectives and

of the salesman's job in order to identify the areas of the job which lend themselves to an incentive approach. Incentive pay is usually most practical where the following conditions exist:
- The sales function involves individual sales rather than a joint effort.
- Sales volume per se is crucial to the success of the business.
- There is little product differentiation.
- The salesman is required to develop potential customers as well as sell them.
- Intangibles such as personal relationships and persuasiveness are crucial.
- The product is not highly technical.
- Preselling through advertising or promotions is not a significant factor in sales transactions.

Level of Total Compensation

The level of total compensation for salesmen is determined primarily by internal pay relationships, competitive market conditions, and the economics of the business. The points of most pertinent comparison inside the company are with sales management positions, administrative sales positions, and positions that have a relationship with or a support function to the sales activity. A second major source of comparison in the company is with the positions from which salesmen might be recruited and those to which they might be promoted. Finally, of course, there is always the general goal of relative equity among all employees within an organization, regardless of practical considerations.

As for comparative pay in the labor market as a whole, an abundance of data is provided by the American Management Association's Executive Compensation Service, by various trade and sales organizations, and by research and consulting organizations. All these studies show, of course, that in any type of sales position, there is considerable variation in the total compensation received by comparable positions in different companies. This is the latitude within which management can exercise discretion.

One important determinant of this discretion should be the economics of the business. Considerations such as break-even points, the profitability of different product lines, identification of the future growth businesses and the growth markets, and the other economic factors will not only influence the nature of the incentive compensation plan, but also, within the perimeter set by the marketplace, affect the level of total compensation.

As far as actual levels of compensation for salesmen are concerned, one published study reports that salesmen earn $5,000 to $150,000 per year, which is accurate but not very helpful. Factors which determine the actual level of total compensation of sales personnel include:

1. *The industry.* Exhibit 21 shows data as of March 1966 on top-level nonsupervisory salesmen in 11 industries, based upon comprehensive studies for companies in these industries.
2. *The job.* Product mix, territorial assignment, and other job-oriented factors largely account for the wide variation of earnings among top men in each industry shown in Exhibit 21.
3. *Form of compensation.* Generally speaking, the higher the percent of incentive compensation to total compensation, the higher the level of total compensation. Valid comparisons of similar jobs in similar industries are difficult to make, but it would appear that men on incentive compensation earn about one-third more than men who are paid a straight salary for similar sales work.

4. *The man.* Nowhere is man worth more intertwined with job worth than in sales positions. A man's sales effectiveness, his following among customers, and other personal abilities also account for a considerable amount of the spread indicated in Exhibit 21.

EXHIBIT 21
SAMPLE EARNINGS OF TOP-LEVEL NONSUPERVISORY SALESMEN
[In thousands of dollars annually. Source: Special surveys in each industry.]

Industry	(March 1966) Average Pay of Top Men	Range of Pay Minimum[1]	Maximum[2]
Building materials	$10	$ 8	$12
Retail sales (stores)	11	7	17
Traffic appliances	11	7	16
Food	12	9	15
Hardware and tools	13	10	18
Industrial components	14	11	17
Pharmaceuticals	14	12	19
Heavy machinery	16	14	22
Primary metals	17	12	20
Computers	21	18	26
Life insurance	22	16	71

[1] Eliminating the lowest-paid 10 percent.
[2] Eliminating the highest-paid 10 percent.
Note: All data rounded to the nearest thousand dollars to avoid suggestion of greater precision than justified.

Determining Base Salaries

Generally speaking, where all the salesman's compensation is in the form of salary, the same considerations which were outlined in the first five chapters are applicable. The only variations will be in format and technique to reflect the unique nature of sales positions. The same is true wherever a significant part of the salesman's compensation is in his base salary. The difference is one of emphasis. More global measures, and more simplified techniques, may be instituted where a large part of the total compensation depends upon incentive earnings.

Use of job evaluation. The majority of companies where base salary is all or a major part of salesmen's total compensation use some form of job evaluation. More often than not, the techniques of evaluation are the standard ones already described, and the same plan which is used to measure administrative, supervisory, and middle management positions is used for sales positions.

Where the basic responsibilities are the same or similar for all sales positions, and the real variations occur in the number of customers, sales volume, and similar objective criteria, pay-grade differentiations can be established through simplified evaluation techniques. Exhibit 22 illustrates a simplified job evaluation program for a metalworking company. This company used the standard evaluation program to relate sales positions to the regular company structure, and salesmen in the various classifications were differentiated as shown in the exhibit.

Merit pay administration. Where only part of the salesman's compensation is in the form of base salary, then it is desirable to differentiate between extra pay through merit increases and extra pay through incentive compensation. While it is difficult to generalize, merit pay administration usually considers increased knowledge, extra experience and skill, long-range demonstrated potential, and general economic factors. Incentive compensation, on the other hand, focuses on specific contributions to the sales effort and to particular sales goals.

In practice, however, merit pay administration and incentive pay are frequently interrelated, and there is an unfortunate tendency to give small merit increases in years

SALESMEN'S COMPENSATION

EXHIBIT 22
SIMPLIFIED POSITION EVALUATION FOR SALES JOBS

Sales Title	Pay Level	Sales Volume	Number of Lines	Persons Supervised Sales	Other
Salesman III	8	Under $500,000	1–3	0	0
Salesman II	10	$500,000 to $2,500,000	3–7	0–1	0
Salesman I	12	$2,500,000 to $5,000,000	All	1–2	0–1
District Manager	14	Over $5,000,000	All	3–10	1–5
Regional Manager	17	Over $20,000,000	All	Over 10	Over 5

of high incentive earnings and vice versa. Conversely, in some plans where incentive pay is geared to base salary, every increase in pay automatically results in an increase in bonus. To the extent possible, sound practice suggests a separation of merit pay increases and incentive pay considerations.

Ground rules and problems. The only special ground rules required in salesmen's salary administration are related either to pay problems inherent in moving a salesman to a different geographical location or to special pay considerations because of his incentive earnings. In many sales forces, it is quite common to move salesmen frequently from one place to another—because of promotions, transfers, or simply reassignments due to changing market conditions. In such cases, special pay adjustments may be necessary owing to cost-of-living considerations or different pay relationships in the new district. Changing a salesman's territory also may call for pay adjustments because his earnings potential from the incentive program is thereby changed.

In some situations, special types of compensation received by a salesman are a significant portion of his total pay. Where this is true, they may also present problems if he is moved from one district to another or from the field to the home office. These special forms of compensation may include an automobile and automobile expenses, cash awards or other prizes from sales contests, expense allowances, membership in clubs, and the opportunity to take an income tax deduction on his home expenses because the salesman uses his home as an office.

Incentive Compensation Plans

Because each must be tailored to the company's products, organization, and other individual circumstances, there are literally thousands of sales incentive compensation plans. Most of these, however, fall into four basic categories: the commission plan, the quota plan, the bonus plan, and the planned-compensation approach.

Commission plans. While the basis may vary, commission plans are those which, in one way or another, relate the salesman's pay directly to his volume of sales. In its simplest form, the salesman is paid X percent of each dollar of sales booked or sales shipped. The rate may vary from a fraction of 1 percent to as much as 25 percent. It may be an increasing percent with increasing volume, a constant percent, or a decreasing one. Frequently, the percentage varies with each product line or service.

Commission plans give the salesman the greatest incentive to sell the largest volume, and this single feature accounts for most of the advantages and disadvantages of such plans. They certainly create the maximum incentive for sales, and also usually provide salesmen with the maximum opportunity for income. In fact, studies indicate that commission salesmen earn about 30 percent more in gross pay than those in comparable jobs who are on straight salary. However, this very focus on sales volume makes it difficult to control sales compensation and sales costs, may not take adequate account of the profitability of different lines or adequate account of sales expense, and certainly encourages salesmen to neglect all duties except those which will result in direct and immediate sales.

Quota system. Quota systems are similar to commission plans except that salesmen are usually paid a salary for a minimum level of sales, which represents their minimum quota, and receive a percent of sales over the quota. Thus, in return for the salary, the company can require a variety of activities—such as customer relations, missionary sales work, and intelligence information from the field—as well as a minimum level of sales. The commission then provides additional incentive to exceed the quota.

The success of such plans usually depends on the correctness of the quota itself. Selling quotas requires an unusual degree of statistical information and knowledge of markets and a precise estimate of sales potential. Quota plans are frequently geared to a district, and the money for extra compensation is accumulated from the sales of all salesmen in the district. The money may then be allocated on a pro rata basis among the salesmen, or it may be apportioned by some appraisal of each man's contribution to the overall achievement.

Bonus plans. Bonus plans may also be geared to the sales a man makes above a given quota. Generally, however, they include such considerations as penetration of market, profit results, and expenses. Like the funds in quota plans, bonus funds are usually accumulated on a group basis and allocated according to individual contribution. Bonus plans take into account more of the variables of sales jobs and salesmen's duties than commission or quota plans, but by the same token their methods of rewarding individual sales personnel are less direct.

Planned compensation. Some plans appear to have the features of either the quota or the bonus, but in fact amount to a planned-compensation approach. This approach is based upon factors such as career compensation progress and appraisal of the individual's potential and contribution. Under it management sets standards as to what an employee's compensation should be and then makes pay and bonus pay judgments which will result in a planned improvement of compensation. Year-to-year variations from the total compensation expected may occur, but these are quickly adjusted, either by salary actions or by adjusting the basis for incentive compensation.

Trends in Incentive Compensation

Various studies over the past 20 years have indicated that there is a trend away from commission plans to bonus, quota, and straight salary plans for salesmen. This does not imply lack of enthusiasm for incentive compensation but rather reflects the fact that a growing number of sales positions do not lend themselves to incentive plans. This, in turn, reflects trends toward a more technological society and more group selling effort.

Partly because of these trends, incentive compensation plans are becoming increasingly complex. They tend to take more things into account, so that payments are based upon qualitative as well as quantitative considerations. Much of this complexity has been made possible by increased technology in market research and use of computers.

Finally, there has been some fundamental new thinking in this area during the past few years. Some companies have instituted what may be labeled the "incremental compensation plan," in which a top salary is paid various personnel for achieving a high level of expectation, and a very high bonus rate is paid for exceeding that high level. In some cases, this bonus is paid in a form which gives salesmen certain tax advantages.

In another plan, regions and districts are literally considered as business enterprises: they almost become distributorships. The company puts up the capital and exercises various controls, as would be expected in any franchised operation, but the people in the district operate almost as a marketing company. The latitude they have is accompanied by considerable responsibility and a greater opportunity to share in the profits of the business. This sharing is sometimes accomplished on a favorable tax basis.

Administration of Sales Compensation Plans

Special administrative requirements of the sales compensation plan include some special problems of communicating the plan to the field sales force, detailed and sometimes extremely complicated record keeping and other administrative chores, and an almost built-in requirement for continuous audit and change.

In some companies, the sales compensation plan must be made so complex that it is difficult to explain to the sales force. If the program is really to relate salesmen's pay to achievement, genuinely motivate salesmen to extend their best efforts, and focus their attention on those things which will promote the achievement of company goals, its structure will necessarily be complicated. Such a program obviously needs considerable explanation, and this task is made more formidable by the typical geographical dispersion of salesmen which forces companies to rely on either written communication or communication through many persons. (Moreover, one study currently under way indicates that although marketing men understand their compensation plan about as well as nonmarketing people, a much higher percentage of them are dissatisfied with it. Thus the problem may be not only one of communication but also one of acceptance.)

The complexity of the compensation system can also make record keeping and other administrative chores extremely burdensome, particularly where payments are related to individual orders and individual accomplishments. Sales compensation plans generally involve a whole bookkeeping operation of their own. From the standpoint of the total company operation, however, this problem amounts to little more than an inconvenience and a minor expense.

The built-in requirement for auditing sales compensation programs and adapting them to changing conditions can be far more costly. One well-known company recently announced that 80 percent of its sales volume in the previous year was based upon products which had been unknown to the firm five years earlier. This extreme case illustrates only one of the many factors which necessitate continual auditing. Basic statistics on earnings, sales by lines, and other indexes of sales activity and effectiveness must be kept up to date. In almost every company, these changing statistics in turn require adjustment of quotas, commission bases, or other elements of the plan—for new products, for changes in customer requirements or locations, for advertising or merchandising methods utilized, and for innumerable other circumstances.

The principal auditor of the sales compensation plan can be the sales supervisor. Frequently one of his principal responsibilities is to make sure that the plan is properly motivating the salesmen—and that the salesmen who are making the biggest contribution are being rewarded with the most compensation. Because of the complexities of such plans and the changes which generally occur every few years, he also has a special responsibility for communicating the details of the program and making sure that his salesmen understand and accept it. Finally, he must be particularly alert to competitive changes in the labor market and changes in the conditions which affect the salesman's job.

CHAPTER VIII

COMPENSATION OF PROFESSIONAL PERSONNEL

WHEN IT COMES TO PERSONNEL ADMINISTRATION AND compensation, the standard assertion is: "Professional people are different." Actually, it is not so much that professional *people* are different as that their *jobs* are different from factory, office, and administrative positions and that compensation administration must be geared to the unique characteristics of these jobs.

Professional Jobs: What They Are

One group of professional jobs might be described as those which require academic knowledge of an advanced type in a recognized field of intellectual study. The nonsupervisory engineer or scientist whose job it is to solve technical problems inherent in design or invention is certainly in this group. Attorneys, economists, physicians, psychologists, and sociologists also fit the definition. Another group of professional jobs requires original and creative work which entails innovation, personal talent, and similar characteristics. Editors, copywriters, and advertising artists fall into this category. Even some staff positions in business planning, finance, and personnel, while they are more craft than profession, have some of the same work characteristics as professional jobs and require the same special compensation considerations.

Professionals typically have wide variety and discretion in terms of the methods they employ, the scheduling of their work, and even the determination of what work is to be done. Choice is the first key to the professional's job: choice of what to do and how to proceed. A second characteristic of the professional is indicated by the term "individual contributor"; his work does not lend itself to a team approach. Third, the imponderable quality of the knowledge and talent which a professional has to sell makes his contribution to the business operation extremely difficult to appraise. A great deal of work has been done in the past few years to develop techniques which solve problems and exploit opportunities in the area of professional compensation. Some of these results are outlined below.

Use of Position Description

Generally speaking, three forms of position descriptions are used for professional jobs: modified functional descriptions, generic descriptions, and simple job titling. Each has been successful in certain conditions. The choice of which to use is based on the degree of professionalism a job has, the number and diversity of professional positions within the firm, and the size, organization, and orientation of the company.

Functional descriptions. The traditional functional position description is one which identifies the various duties of the job. The first difficulty with such an approach in professional jobs is that descriptions of jobs within a given discipline read about the same. For example, electronic design engineers are engineers who design electronic components; the only difference between the beginner and advanced engineer is in the complexity of the electronic component they design. As a result, descriptions of different levels of this work may simply involve strings of increasingly superlative adjectives.

The second problem with the functional position description is that the assignments given to professional employees usually depend somewhat upon such factors as personal ability, experience, career development, and department scheduling. Also, the types of assignments may vary greatly in a rather short period. At one time, for instance, an engineer may be doing extremely complex design work; yet a few days later he may be assigned a design drafting chore.

Because of these characteristics of professional jobs, functional position descriptions for professionals are most applicable where there is a steady flow of work and where the descriptions deal mainly with the differences between disciplines rather than those within a discipline. Even so, companies which have successfully used functional descriptions have found it necessary to do three things: (1) confine the description of work to the highest-level, most complex, and most professionally advanced duties that are involved; (2) prepare a glossary of terms which give body and substance to the superlative adjectives; and (3) provide many examples of the type of work usually assigned.

Generic descriptions. These descriptions do not even attempt to describe job assignments in a professional position but rather seek to define in very broad terms the level of professional work involved. As shown in Exhibit 23, the generic description is relatively simple to write and need only be done once. The writer, however, must have some knowledge of the field and must understand what constitutes various levels of professional competence. The generic approach certainly provides needed flexibility and eliminates the great cost and sometimes great frustration of attempting to write and rewrite functional descriptions.

EXHIBIT 23
A GENERIC JOB DESCRIPTION

Title: Senior Engineer

Description: Performs a full range of engineering work, including assignments requiring special engineering qualifications or attainments in fields where precedents are not clearly defined. Initiative and judgment are expected with only limited guidance from others. Accountable for quality, accuracy, and planning of own work or for work of other engineers. Completed assignments subject to limited review of overall results.

It also recognizes that the value of professional employees must be determined basically through an analysis of individual capabilities. The very flexibility of the approach, however, causes considerable difficulties in administration. Generic descriptions are so broad in scope and general in content that they do not always serve as a meaningful guide in decision making. Also, the fact that professional employees are assigned to levels on the basis of what they can do rather than what they actually do may result in payment by the company for services not performed.

Job titling. This in effect is the same as the generic approach, except that it does not even call for a written description of the various levels of the profession. It provides maximum flexibility, but in this approach all the drawbacks of the generic method are intensified.

Use of Job Evaluation

Even though it is difficult to separate man worth from job worth in professional positions, some basis for assigning relative value to professional jobs is useful in pay decisions. Several of the most widely used methods are described below.

Standard job evaluations. Many companies rely on the standard job evaluation approach to establish pay grades for professional positions. If job evaluation is to be applied to professional positions, two basic requirements are essential to success. The first is, of course, that descriptions must be realistic, whether they are functional descriptions or generic descriptions. The second is that the job evaluation plan itself must be appropriate. Many evaluation plans fail to measure professional jobs adequately because they are primarily designed for production and administrative positions and so lean heavily on such considerations as dollars of assets, volumes of sales, budgets, and numbers of people supervised. Such plans simply cannot give appropriate weighting, either in terms of values within the business or in terms of values in the marketplace, to positions whose key factors are essentially knowledge and talent.

Where these tests are met, job evaluation has served as a useful guide in pay decisions for professional employees. "Usefulness" can, however, be a relative term. Because of the greater complexity, the individualized nature, and the many intangible considerations of professional jobs, evaluation results are undoubtedly less precise than with other types of positions.

Generic classifications. Companies which use generic job descriptions for professional employees frequently divide these jobs into four to six generic levels and then classify them into the company pay structure. Usually the slotting is managed so that the maximum of one level overlaps the minimum of the next higher level. In this way, a professional person moves smoothly from one pay level to the next as he progresses in his field.

This approach is really the classification method of job

PROFESSIONAL PERSONNEL

evaluation in the sense that a position, however described, is classified into an existing pay level. However, it has two important differences from the classification system. First, since there are no definitions of the pay levels, generic classification provides no real management guide except the money involved. This can invite salary accommodation rather than salary administration. Second, companies which use the approach are really classifying individuals rather than positions.

Career-curve approach. The so-called career-curve approach is a method specifically developed for professional jobs, particularly in engineering. In essence, it assumes that after they finish their education, professional employees will develop within their disciplines at some standard rate as a result of their experience in the field. This assumed progress is shown as a curve such as those in the first graph of Exhibit 24, where the average earnings of various groups of professionals surveyed are plotted against the number of years since they received their degree.

Under this approach, position descriptions—if they are used at all—are not basic to the salary administration process. Determination of salaries becomes a simple matter of looking up the number of years since an employee received his degree and then reading off the salary indicated by the curve. Generally, however, it is recognized that professionals with the same years of experience will vary in their ability. As a result, a number of curves usually are drawn representing different levels of proficiency. Then it is the job of the supervisor to judge the level of each employee and to determine his salary by following the curve to the appropriate year since degree.

The validity of this approach depends, first, upon the supervisor's ability to place each individual in the correct curve and, second, upon the correctness of the curves

EXHIBIT 24
Professional Maturity Curves

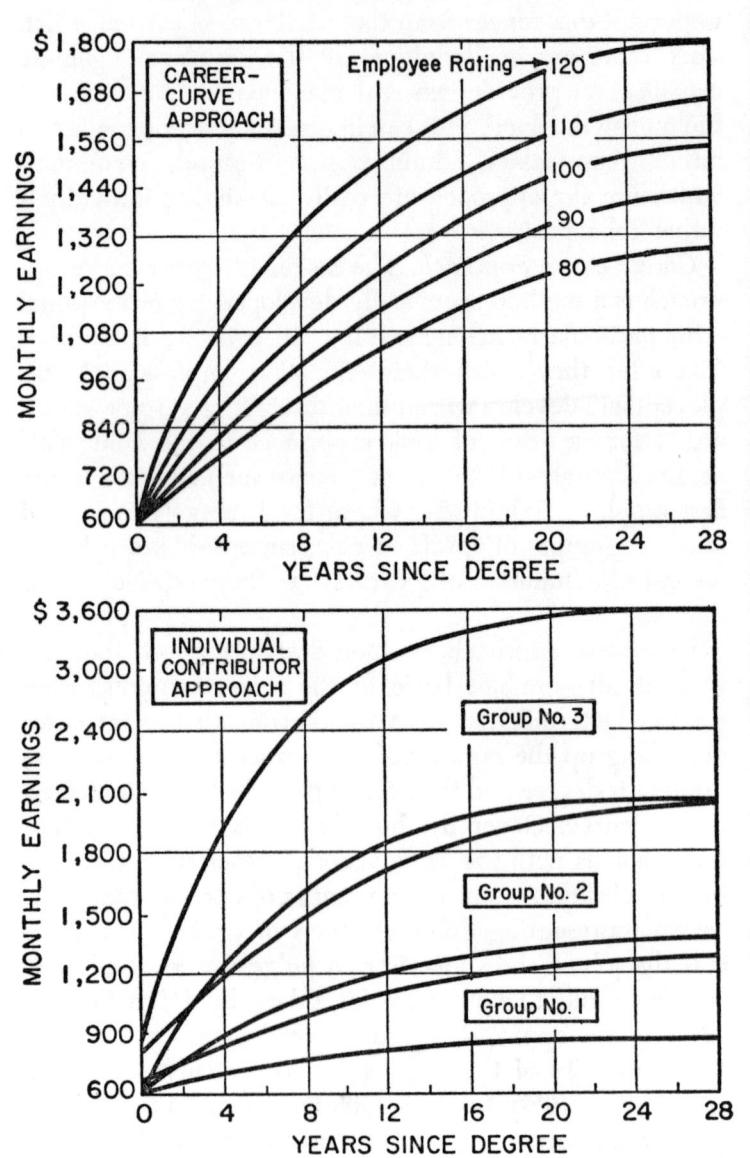

themselves. Placing people on the correct maturity curve is strictly a matter of performance—thus it is another form of merit rating. Unless it is done well, the process can become a mere rationalization of predetermined increases. So far as the correctness of the curves themselves is concerned, it is certainly questionable whether we can assume that all engineering employees progress in a uniform way. Actually, an analysis of the data which goes to make up the curves indicates that there is no such thing as average progress. The curves represent the "best fit" of widely dispersed salary figures in each year since degree. This in itself indicates a widely varying rate of progress among individual professional employees.

The greatest advantage claimed for the career-curve approach is that it concentrates managers' thinking on individual progress and contribution. The method is certainly a less complicated process, involving less administrative effort, than standard job evaluation. Also, its automatic aspects have somewhat the same appeal for a few professionals and their supervisors that seniority pay increases have for production employees.

It should be noted that, in fact, the career-curve method is essentially the same as the traditional job evaluation approach. The only difference between the two is that the horizontal coordinate in Exhibit 24 measures years since degree, whereas in the traditional salary structure approach this coordinate measures job evaluation points. Of course, the career curves are regressive instead of progressive, but this primarily reflects the fact that the curves are usually applied only to nonsupervisory engineers.

In summary, it can be said that the career-curve approach, with a number of embellishments, has proved to be a practical, though far from perfect, method of salary administration in large engineering organizations that are essentially advanced research and development groups. In other cases, the approach is probably not adequate as a basic technique for wage and salary administration. Career curves can, however, serve as supplemental guides for pay decisions made under a standard position evaluation program, a generic classification program, or an administered program.

Individual-contribution approach. While there are a number of variations of the individual-contribution approach, they are identical in that they abandon any attempt to describe or evaluate jobs. Instead, they place the entire emphasis upon the individual's personal contribution and his potential.

One such approach utilized in some engineering laboratories is illustrated in the second graph of Exhibit 24. In the example shown, three broad levels of engineering competency and proficiency were defined without regard to years of experience. For each a range of value rather than a simple career curve was established. Within five years after an engineer completes his education, his performance and capabilities are carefully appraised, and he is placed in one of the three groups. His salary is then planned within the range of curves assigned to the group. In this way attention is concentrated upon the individual salary progress of each engineer. In addition, managers making salary decisions can consider all important factors by using the salary planning practices already described.

A second form of the individual-contribution approach is really a resurgence of individual bargaining. Some scientists, commercial artists, lawyers, economists, and other professionals are so well known and so highly respected, or can make such a tremendous personal contribution, that their value defies any method of salary classification. They are indeed worth what it takes to get them. Some companies that have been confronted with a number of such cases have developed systematic methods for analyzing their situation and the values involved. These methods have not been determinants or guides to decisions but rather yardsticks for individual bargaining.

Salary Structures for Professional Employees

Professional salary structures may take the traditional form, with pay minimums and maximums; may utilize some systematic method of individualized pay ranges; or may be based on career curves. In each case, there are two questions involved: how to price the levels and how to develop the structure itself. In the event that a separate structure is developed for professionals, there is the additional question of integrating this structure with those in effect for other groups of employees.

Pricing pay levels. As with any other pay structure, setting professional salary levels involves considerations of company economic and operating factors, company employment experience, and data gained from market surveys. In pricing enginering positions, primary reliance is usually placed on the survey, and this is becoming increasingly true of other types of professional work. The reason is the continuing shortage of high-level professional employees, which leads to an emphasis upon setting competitive pay levels that can attract and retain qualified people.

In surveys of professional pay levels, however, selecting the right companies and the right jobs to study is far more difficult than in surveys of the pay received by other types of employees. The professional tends to identify himself and his career interests more with his field of work than with any individual employer or industry. This means that many kinds of companies in many geographic areas are really market competitors, and that there is a bewildering array of labor markets and competitive conditions for different professional positions. Too, the very difficulty of defining duties (discussed earlier in this chapter) increases the difficulty of making comparisons with professional positions in other companies. As a result, the effort and cost involved in assuring competitiveness of salary levels for professional jobs are considerably more than in most other types of positions. Two data sources are commonly used: (1) broad-coverage general surveys of professional work, such as those conducted by the American Management Association's Executive Compensation Service and the U.S. Bureau of Labor Statistics; and (2) specific salary surveys within the profession, such as the studies conducted by professional associations and those made by various companies on a joint basis.

Integrating pay structures. Most companies have found it not only possible but practical to develop one structure for all groups of employees. There was a trend a number of years ago to establish separate structures for each group, but it arose because inappropriate techniques were being used for position description writing, job evaluation, and surveying rather than because the approach was inherently desirable. Where appropriate techniques are utilized, it is usually feasible to incorporate pay levels for professionals, along with other groups into one structure.

When this is not possible, or where there may be special administrative reasons for establishing a separate professional structure, the dual-structure system must be utilized. The example given in Exhibit 25 shows 6 levels of professional work covering a spread in pay from $7,300 to $33,700 and 18 levels of exempt classifications with a spread of $6,000 to $40,500. Professional level I extends from the minimum of exempt level 3 to the maximum of exempt level 4, professional level II from the minimum of

EXHIBIT 25: PARALLEL SALARY STRUCTURE

	Professional Salary Structure					Exempt Salary Structure		
Level	Typical Position	Minimum Pay	Maximum Pay		Level	Typical Position	Minimum Pay	Maximum Pay
I	Associate engineer	$7,300	$10,800		1	Trainee	$6,000	$8,100
					2	Assistant foreman	6,600	8,900
II	Assistant engineer	8,800	13,100		3	Junior accountant	7,300	9,800
	Assistant economist				4	Admin. asst. (engineering)	8,000	10,800
III	Engineer	10,600	15,800		5	Foreman	8,800	11,900
	Artist				6	Accountant	9,700	13,100
	Attorney				7	General foreman	10,600	14,300
	Psychologist				8	Industrial engineer	11,700	15,800
IV	Senior engineer	12,800	19,000		9	Plant personnel supervisor	12,800	17,300
	Plant physician				10	Engineering section manager	14,100	19,000
	Economist							
V	Scientist	15,500	25,300		11	Manager quality control	15,500	21,000
	Tax attorney				12	Engineering department manager	17,000	23,000
	Consulting psychologist				13	Controller	18,700	25,300
VI	Senior scientist	20,600	33,700		14	Laboratory manager	20,600	27,800
					15	Corporate insurance dir.	22,600	30,400
					16	Director of engineering	25,000	33,700
					17	Division president	27,400	37,000
					18	Executive vice president	30,000	40,500

PROFESSIONAL PERSONNEL 187

level 5 to the maximum of level 6, and so forth. When the structures are related, the progress of the professional person matches that of his colleagues in supervisory, line, and staff work. Parallel structures such as this also make it possible to transfer persons from professional to administrative or management positions.

Administration of Professional Salaries

In addition to all the general considerations outlined in Chapter V on salary administration, pay decisions regarding professional employees involve some special problems. One concerns the relationship between money and motivation for professional employees. Although it is certainly not correct to think that money is unimportant to professionals, it can be said that in a large number of cases achievement of extraordinarily high earnings is not their main consideration. These are difficult matters requiring considerably more research, but the following generalizations are probably pertinent.

Except for those who are clearly aiming for the management of professional work and eventually for a general management position, high income expectations are not paramount in the minds of professionals. Their striving is directed toward producing high-caliber professional work and advancing in the professional field. However, the professional worker expects pay progress and equitable treatment and can, like any employee, become very dissatisfied if he does not receive them. Whereas the desire for money may not motivate him to increase production, lack of financial progress or inequitable treatment can contribute to less productiveness.

A second special problem of salary administration for professionals is the general need for greater delegation of salary decisions to the individual supervisor. This, of course, is because many of the factors involved in pay questions are related to technical matters requiring intimate knowledge of the professional field. Only a lawyer, for instance, can judge the excellence of a legal recommendation.

Frequently, owing to particular professional orientations and habits of thought, there is some difference in emphasis on technique in salary administration for professionals. To take an overgeneralized example, engineers tend to be analytical and precise and to approach the salary structure in terms of charts, complicated scales, and rather sophisticated numerical rankings and weightings. If these techniques become a substitute for good judgment, then there is a danger; if, on the other hand, they assist the supervisor of professionals to make decisions and lead his subordinates to greater acceptance of these decisions, they are appropriate.

Special Compensation for Professionals

There are a number of nonsalary items which may represent real costs to the company and real income values to the professional:

- Patent recognition.
- Encouragement, support, and compensation for publication in professional journals.
- Special bonuses for inventions, important research, or major solutions of company problems.
- Membership in professional organizations or attendance at professional meetings.
- Encouragement, time off, and financial support for additional education.
- Better facilities—which may include not only labora-

tory facilities but better office space and more technical assistance.
- Greater flexibility as to hours of work and location of work.

Although such items complicate pay administration, they are usually vital to proper compensation and motivation of professional employees. Therefore, they provide important opportunities for better utilization of professional talent within the company.

CHAPTER IX

SUPERVISORY, TECHNICAL, AND ADMINISTRATIVE PERSONNEL

SUPERVISORY, TECHNICAL, AND ADMINISTRATIVE POSITIONS, though very different, are grouped together because they do have one thing in common: They are all intermediate groups. Supervisory employees have an intermediate position between management and nonsupervisory personnel; administrative employees fall between office and top-level staff; and technical employees occupy a place between skilled production workers and professional employees.

SUPERVISORY EMPLOYEES

Since supervisors are the first line of management, it is primarily they who explain and administer the salary program of the company to its nonsupervisory employees. How they apply the program and how they explain it essentially determine how the rank and file sees it. By the same token, however, salary administration is applied to supervisors. How well they understand what it means to them, and how reasonable its provisions concerning their own salaries appear to them, certainly will influence how they administer and explain the program to their subordinates.

The Supervisory Group

As used here, the term "supervisors" means employees who are organizationally no more than one or two levels removed from nonsupervisory personnel. They do not set policy but carry it out—essentially, by having others perform work. Thus supervision itself is a major part of their responsibilities, and they generally have at least a half-dozen subordinates over whom they exercise authority in the traditional "hire or fire" meaning. Finally, they are so intimately involved in the assignment of work, the training of personnel, the solution of daily operating problems, and assistance to subordinates in their work that they must have, in considerable depth, a technical knowledge of the jobs which they supervise.

In this section, therefore, we are considering the supervisor in the classic sense: the person whose activities are almost exclusively concentrated on work assignment, training, and control over the work of nonsupervisory personnel. There are other employees who also supervise, but in these cases the supervision itself is a small part of the overall responsibility. An example is an engineering section leader who may have three or four persons working for him but whose main value is his professional knowledge and the professional work he performs personally. The definition of "supervisor" used here also excludes persons who have only limited supervisory responsibility, such as group leaders.

Descriptions and Position Evaluation

Probably nine-tenths of all supervisory positions are covered by position descriptions and classified by some form of job evaluation. These techniques have been found quite satisfactory in salary administration for supervisors; the only question is what system works best. Many companies have learned from bad experience that it is usually unwise to merely extend the office or production position evaluation programs upward to cover supervisory employees. Almost invariably, it is more prudent to apply the program for management and administrative personnel to the supervisory group.

Usually supervisory positions are not difficult to evaluate, provided position descriptions contain adequate information in the first place. Descriptions should not only outline job responsibilities but also cover topics such as these:

1. Scope data, including number of persons supervised, asset value of equipment, supplies and equipment utilized, and dollar amount of budgets.
2. Latitude of action or authority possessed by the supervisor.
3. Additional nonsupervisory relationships required with people both inside and outside the company.
4. Climate of the job, including such intangibles as goals and objectives, conditions under which work must be performed, and rate of change.

Factors Affecting Pay Levels

All positions, including supervisory jobs, are affected to some extent by both market and administrative factors. Market factors, however, are not very strong so far as supervisory positions are concerned, because most supervisors are either selected from those supervised or transferred from other positions within the company. This means that the "market" for supervisory jobs is primarily the company's own manpower reservoir. The absence of strong market pressures, together with the intermediate position which supervisors occupy betwen management and nonsupervisory workers means that internal comparisons are the primary determinant of supervisors' pay levels.

In addition to job evaluation, probably the most important internal pay comparison for supervisory positions is the relationship between the pay of the supervisor and that of his subordinates. This is a key comparison. Inadequate pay differentials between the supervisor and his subordinate employees obviously pose a major problem, for they undermine the morale of the supervisor and make it difficult for the company to move its best men into supervisory positions.

Various rules of thumb have been evolved by companies to help in judging what constitutes satisfactory differentials between supervisors and their subordinates. Usually no single guide is adequate, and certainly none should be followed without judgment and discretion. Following are five general criteria:

1. The supervisor's pay grade should be at least two levels higher than the grade of the highest-rated job he supervises. In practice, he is usually classified 3 to 5 pay levels higher.
2. The supervisor's base salary should be at least 15 percent higher than the straight-time earnings of the highest-paid subordinate.
3. The supervisor's gross pay (including bonuses and any overtime compensation) should be at least 10 percent higher than the gross pay (including overtime) of the highest-paid subordinate.
4. The gross pay of the supervisor should be at least 25 percent more than the average gross pay of all subordinates.
5. The gross pay of the supervisor should be no more

than 75 percent higher than the average gross pay of all subordinates.

The Problem of Introducing Incentive

Various studies have demonstrated that salary practices for supervisors are more closely related to salary practices for office and production employees than to those for management employees. Patterns of average increases and dispersion of increases for supervisors resemble those for production and office employees. Even the procedures and techniques used for administering supervisors' salaries tend to be closer to plant or office procedures than to managerial or professional methods.

These conditions are not what management seeks, or what should be, but rather what actually exists. Most companies, for instance, wish to inject more incentive into pay practices for supervisors by gearing increases to differences in performance. Most wish to bring supervisory salary administration in general closer to practices for management and higher-level staff positions. Certainly they recognize that the absence of a true merit approach reduces the incentive for supervisors to put forth their best efforts and that automatic increases tend to make them think more like nonsupervisory groups than like management.

To have a genuine merit program for supervisors first requires that responsibility, authority, and decision making be built into supervisory positions. Otherwise, these jobs will not be evaluated at a high enough level to permit meaningful differentiations based upon performance or anything else. If a more responsible position is developed at the supervisory level, the company must staff the job with persons of high caliber and take steps to give them the incentive, the leadership, and the training to perform effectively. Finally, to have a merit program for supervisors, management must observe the performance of supervisory personnel carefully and discriminate clearly in favor of those who perform well.

The Problem of Overtime Compensation

In companies which do not have or cannot build meaningful differentials between the pay of supervisors and that of their subordinates, the problem of overtime compensation for supervisors is pressing and difficult. Where employees are required to work significant amounts of overtime during the year, and where the supervisor must work essentially the same time as those supervised, gross pay inequities are inevitable unless the supervisors' base pay is sufficiently high or unless they receive extra pay for extraordinarily long work hours.

Many companies do nothing about the problem. Most of these recognize that a problem exists, but they are afraid that paying supervisors for overtime might lead them to work themselves or their departments unnecessarily long hours in order to get the extra pay. Also, some companies are concerned about the administrative and other problems which might arise from giving supervisors overtime pay. There are other firms which believe that the indirect values in a supervisory job, such as prestige and security, provide an indirect form of income. And, while few will say so, there are probably some which are aware of the problem but are convinced that the supervisors will accept the situation.

Undoubtedly, the actual cost of paying supervisors for overtime is a consideration in many companies. It is difficult to visualize cost as a major problem, however, when the company is already paying overtime for those supervised. In thinking about costs of extra compensation for supervisors it is important to consider the effects of lowered morale, and perhaps lowered efficiency, because of what supervisors may rightly view as pay inequities.

Some companies, of course, do nothing about overtime compensation simply because there is little overtime worked. Others which have intermittent or seasonal overtime work do not pay supervisors overtime because the very production workers who receive the overtime pay frequently are laid off during the course of the year and therefore have offsetting "undertime" pay. Still other companies handle the situation by giving supervisors compensatory time off when business slows down.

At the other extreme are companies which pay supervisors premium overtime rates for each hour worked beyond the standard work week. This does indeed solve pay and equity problems for the supervisor. Unfortunately, though, it sometimes merely transfers them to a higher level. Also, it may encourage supervisors to work themselves and their subordinates longer hours, or at least it may discourage them from tightly controlling overtime work. Finally, such premium payments have the effect of grouping supervisors with production workers instead of with management.

An increasing number of companies follow a middle course: They allow some extra compensation, but it is less than premium rates and is paid only under prescribed conditions. Many companies, for instance, will not pay overtime or extra compensation for intermittent overtime or for overtime which is less than 45 or even 50 hours per week. Many pay straight time for extra hours, and some pay only a part of straight time. Except in extreme cases, these practices preserve reasonable pay differentials in a manner which protects the supervisor's identity and avoids the possibility of abuses.

Exhibit 26 illustrates the effect of four typical extra-compensation plans for supervisors in maintaining supervisor/supervised pay relationships. In each case, it was assumed that the gross pay of the supervisor was $7,000 per year and the straight-time pay of the subordinates was $6,000.

Without any overtime, the gross pay relationships be-

EXHIBIT 26
PAY RELATIONSHIPS UNDER VARIOUS OVERTIME-PAY PROVISIONS FOR SUPERVISORS

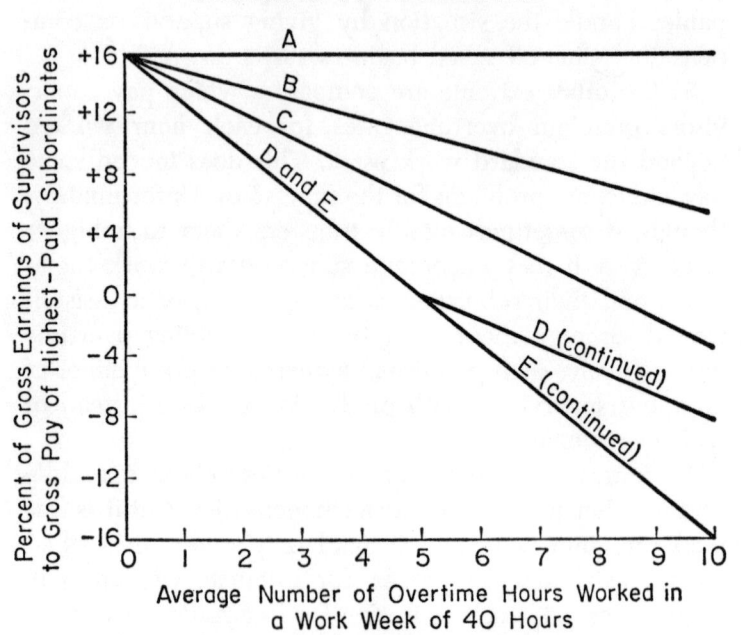

A Time and one-half over 40 hours per week
B Straight time over 40 hours per week
C Half-time over 40 hours per week
D Straight time over 45 hours per week
E No overtime for supervisors

come inadequate even when a few hours of overtime are worked. Also, any corridor provision, such as straight-time pay over 45 hours, yields inadequate supervisor-subordinate pay differentials unless these differentials are quite high to begin with. Unless they are high, Exhibit 26 shows, some form of extra compensation from the first hour of overtime worked is essential.

Bonus Payments for Supervisors

About one-fourth of all companies which do not provide overtime compensation for supervisors have a modified premium pay policy in the form of bonus payments to supervisors. Surveys indicate that about half of these bonus plans are a part of the overall management profit-sharing or incentive compensation plan. The yield for supervisors is usually about a month's pay. The difficulty with such profit-based plans is, of course, that while we would normally expect profits to be high in the years when supervisors have worked extra time, it does not necessarily turn out this way.

Probably the most typical supervisory bonus plan calls for discretionary payment to supervisors. Once management decides that a bonus is to be paid, each individual's share is determined by pay level, by years of service, by extra hours worked, by performance, or by any combination of these or other factors. Such a plan obviously gives management great flexibility. On the other hand, it may not solve any pay problem or serve any purpose. Certainly the basis of payment must be a mystery to the recipient. Such plans do not cost much, but, unless carefully administered and explained, they can mean considerable trouble.

Only about 2 percent of companies have special supervisory incentive compensation plans directly related to the various responsibilities assigned to the supervisor. The reason for this low percentage is not lack of enthusiasm but rather lack of practical ways to implement such a program. A growing number of companies, however, are seeking to develop compensation plans for all levels of employees which would relate extra compensation to genuine achievement. Practical difficulties they must solve include establishing meaningful and equitable formulas, developing the statistics necessary for such plans, and determining base standards.

Where bonus plans for supervisors do exist, usually they either are related to budget or cost data or involve special awards for special achievements.

At this time, some major companies are conducting computer-based research to devise methods for gearing incentive compensation plans to specific accountabilities for supervisors, and for other groups of employees as well. Concrete results are not yet available, but tentative conclusions seem most promising.

TECHNICAL EMPLOYEES

In many companies, there is a broad group of technical employees who occupy a position between the professional and the skilled production workers. These are the subprofessional personnel. Their exact jobs vary with the profession: in economics, the subprofessional may be the statistician; in engineering, he is the technician or the draftsman.

Because technical employees have a close relationship with professionals, and because their own work is subprofessional, a modified form of the professional salary administration policies outlined in Chapter VIII is appropriate for use with subprofessional personnel. In describing technical positions, for instance, either modified functional descriptions or generic descriptions are suitable. As with professional positions, it is important to be assured that the position evaluation plan, if used, gives adequate weighting to knowledge and skill. Some companies have successfully utilized either generic-classification systems or career-curve methods for technical persons.

Overtime compensation also can become a special problem with technical employees. Many of them are clearly within the requirements of the Fair Labor Standards Act and therefore must be paid overtime compensation. Others may be exempt but are at such an income level that they should at least be considered for overtime compensation, both for reasons of equity and to preserve the company's internal pay relationships. With technical personnel, the problem of overtime compensation is one of control. Frequently, technicians work in small groups and are closely involved with the work of the professionals. The professionals may put in long hours, either because of work pressure or because of attachment to their profession. Since they are not paid overtime, it is often difficult and perhaps unwise to restrict their hours. If it is necessary to have technicians work with them, however, there is built-in uncontrollable overtime compensation for the technician. Experience generally indicates that the control in this situation must come from day-to-day common sense in administration rather than from any set of rules.

Probably the most difficult problem in salary administration for the technician, and one which is becoming more prevalent in our increasingly technological society, stems from this very relationship to the professional man. To some extent, the technician's real role is to do work which the professional could do himself but which would prevent him from concentrating on higher-level activities.

The technician can thus conserve the time and increase the productiveness of the professional and by this support can make him more effective. Since some of the value of the technician is related to the value of the professional, the technician may be undervalued, if we appraise only his prescribed duties and discount his support value. Furthermore, unless compensation administration does recognize the importance of such support it may actually discourage the technician from becoming more effective in backing up the professional, even when this is his most valuable activity.

The final problem of salary administration for technical employees is the very fact that the number, diversity, and job levels of technicians are growing rapidly. As each new professional discipline and new specialized technical staff position is added to the company payroll, the need for subprofessionals is expanding on a geometric basis. Also, faced with a continuing shortage of professional personnel, alert companies are finding more and more ways in which technicians can relieve the professional shortage by assuming work that has formerly been done by the professional. This results not only in an increasing number of technicians but also in an upgrading of their skill and levels of responsibility.

ADMINISTRATIVE EMPLOYEES

The only common characteristic shared by jobs in the administrative group is that they do not fit into management, supervisory, professional, sales, technical, production, or office groups. They usually fall within the top two or three pay levels for nonexempt jobs and within the five to eight lowest pay grades among exempt ones. Except for such minor resemblances, there are more dissimilarities than similarities among administrative positions. Thus there are no guides that fit all the employees who fall into this category; it is best only to specify particular administrative jobs and outline special problems involved with each.

Secretaries to members of top management represent one type of employee in the administrative group. Their true relation to the senior executive is much like the technician's relation to the professional, for although they perform various mechanical duties, their primary function is to conserve the executive's time and to help him perform his job better. This suggests that salary treatment of executive secretaries should be similar to that of the technician.

A second type of administrative position is held by the trainee or bright young man who is being groomed for future high-level responsibilities. Here the problem is that the position which the young man now holds may have no relation to his real value. Frequently trainees are rotated in jobs to give them a diversity of experience, and the training nature of their assignments means that their actual responsibility must be somewhat limited. By the same token, however, the trainee's long-range value to the company is great, and the caliber of the person is high. For these few but highly important employees, salary administration policies used for other groups will not be appropriate. They must literally be exempted from any system, and their salaries must progress sufficiently to attract them to the company in the first place and also to retain them.

At the opposite extreme is the senior clerk—the long-service employee who has come up in an operation such as accounting or statistics. Because of his detailed knowledge of the department, he has assumed levels of responsibility beyond the clerical scope. The problems here may be threefold. First, such an employee may have intangible value not easily recorded in a position description or evaluated by any system. He may, for example, give advice based on the way a certain event was handled many years ago; he may be the only person who remembers where things are or who did what; or he may have a great store of information on company procedures. Second, such persons frequently are paid some premium unrelated to the job, simply as a reward for especially long service. Third, even without such premiums for long service, they may finally achieve a salary level which is so high in relation to the duties they perform that additional increases are difficult to justify, although the increases are difficult not to grant.

These are only a few illustrations of the types and diversity of problems in salary administration for the administrative group. A comprehensive list would include dozens of special cases. For the great majority of administrative positions, however, the methods described in the first five chapters are applicable.

CHAPTER X

SALARY ADMINISTRATION FOR MANAGEMENT

SALARY ADMINISTRATION FOR THE MANAGEMENT GROUP IS particularly complex, involving difficult and sometimes controversial questions. As the number and diversity of management positions continue to grow, these questions will undoubtedly become more complex and their satisfactory solution more and more important to the success of an enterprise.

The Management Group

While each company has its own definition of "management," the term generally refers to those positions in which the decisions made have a significant impact upon overall company profitability. The management group usually represents about 1 percent of the total employment of the company, although the percentage will tend to be larger than this in small companies, in companies with a high capital investment, in those with a very rapid growth rate, in those with a high mix of exempt employees, in those which are highly decentralized.

Management jobs, of course, are those at the top of the

business hierarchy. Exhibit 27 illustrates a conventional company structure and shows how the groups of employees generally fit together within it. The very identification of these groups is one of the difficult tasks of salary administration in the modern enterprise. Also, the differences between jobs in various groups are frequently difficult to distinguish, there are overlaps between groups,

EXHIBIT 27
EMPLOYEE GROUPS

[Pyramid diagram with labels: Executive, Higher Management, Middle Management, Professional, Sales, Supervisory and Administrative, Technical, Production and Office]

and problems of "interface" inevitably arise. The ideal pay program provides for the different needs and characteristics of the group within the company hierarchy, yet forms an integrated salary administration operation. As shown in Exhibit 28, many companies have approached this problem by devising a continuous structure from the lowest-rated job to the highest. Note that there is considerable overlapping in pay between the various groups.

EXHIBIT 28
An Integrated Salary Structure

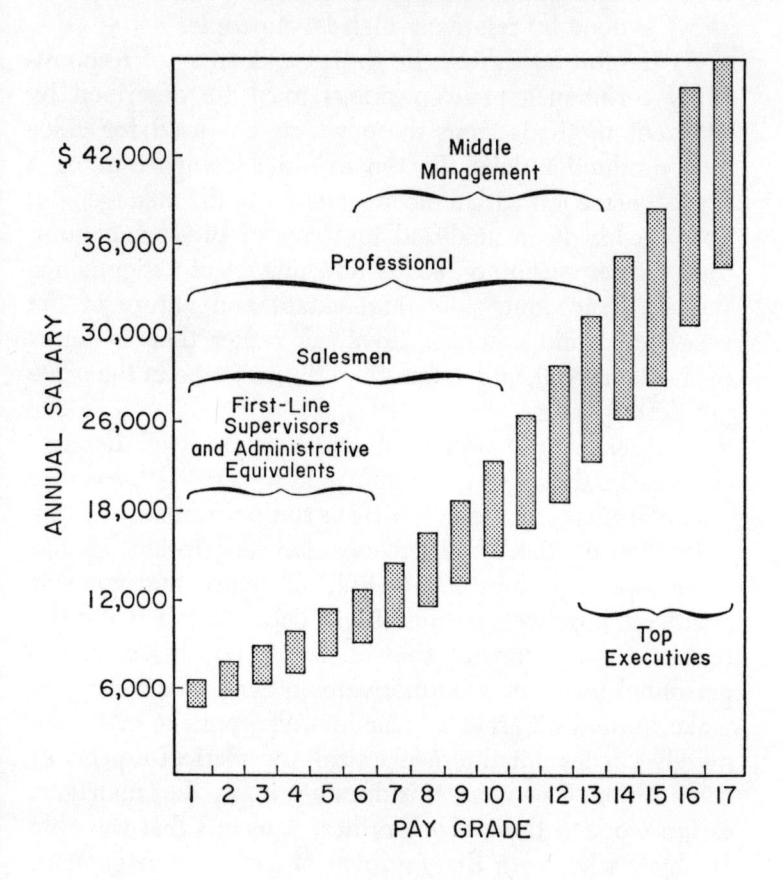

Adapting Job Descriptions to Managers

Description of management-level positions is extremely difficult, costly, and time consuming. In a changing business, management position descriptions must be constantly rewritten because organizational or operational changes are continually affecting one or more managerial jobs.

Also, demanding technical requirements inherent in writing descriptions for management make it necessary that they be done by relatively high-level people.

As Exhibit 29 shows, the duties and areas of responsibility for management positions must be described by different methods from those which are used for office and production jobs. In the exhibit's comparison of a typical office job with a management job, the management position has been analyzed in terms of broad functions, areas of responsibility, scope and impact of assignments, degree of accountability, and extent and nature of the supervision and influence involved, rather than in terms of the detailed listing of tasks and duties found in the office job description.

Another unique aspect of management-level descriptions is the difficulty encountered in separating the duties which are assigned to a job from the performance of the individual on the job. In theory, job descriptions should be completely impersonal. But, in many management positions, how well an individual does his job really determines the nature of the job itself. For instance, the personnel manager who motivates others effectively may make quite a different job for himself from the man who merely carries out the mechanical and clerical aspects of the position. Of course, this does not imply that managers assign work to themselves; rather, it means that the able manager who, with the approval of higher management, absorbs greater responsibility has in effect changed the nature of his job.

Because of the time and cost involved in writing management position descriptions, many companies have come to the conclusion that they should be prepared primarily for management purposes. Under this approach, they become basically a management tool used in assigning

EXHIBIT 29
INHERENT DIFFERENCES IN WORK ASSIGNMENTS

[Management vs. nonmanagement positions]

Analysis of Assignment in Terms of:	Typical Office Job	Typical Management Job
Skill	Largely mechanical skills.	Nonmechanical skills such as leadership; organizing ability; ability to coordinate, guide, and control the work of others.
Knowledge	Technical knowledge; knowledge of routine procedures; specific knowledge of "how to do" mechanical or procedural tasks.	Depth and breadth of knowledge of some aspect of company work, field of business, etc. Understanding as well as knowhow.
Responsibility	Responsibility largely for accuracy and technical correctness of own work.	General responsibility for results.
Decision making or judgment	"Task" decisions: Is their work correct or not correct? Should they refer to supervisor or go ahead?	Frequent decisions of a somewhat limited nature but affecting a section of the business and the work of others.
Planning	Some planning of timing and sequence of own work. Prescribed work procedures restrict areas of planning.	Largely plans own work. Plans directly affect or influence work of others. Planning for new and better methods.
Conditions of work	Concentration; noise, heat, dirt, physical effort; surroundings.	Conditions, as such, not a consideration.
Initiative	Largely specific work assignments; standardized procedures; initiative largely confined to how quickly tasks are performed.	Only broad objectives; high degree of freedom to follow own methods, initiate changes, and so on.
Supervision	None.	A basic aspect of the job.
Influence	Little, aside from suggestions and relationships with other employees working in group.	A basic aspect of the job.

work, communicating responsibilities, establishing authority limits, setting performance standards, and reviewing the performance of management. Descriptions which are good enough to serve these purposes are more than adequate for use in job evaluation. They will also serve other broad functions: for instance, they can be valuable aids in organizational planning, manpower planning, staffing, and management development.

With these management purposes in mind, an increasing number of companies are utilizing questionnaire techniques in preparing management-level descriptions. The very exercise involved in having the manager think through his own responsibilities and articulate them can be helpful. Certainly having him review the completed questionnaire with immediate supervising management can clarify areas of responsibility and assure understanding of what is expected in the job.

Management position descriptions must provide more than an outline of duties and responsibilities if they are to serve broad management purposes, salary administration objectives, or management development, staffing, and organizational planning ends. Either the position descriptions themselves or supplemental manuals should supply pertinent information on such aspects of business as the following:

- Products, operational methods, management practices, distributive systems, and the like.
- Essential characteristics of the company and principal problem areas confronting it.
- Plans and forecasts, such as those represented in five-year plans.
- Organizational charts covering all management levels.
- Nature and extent of competitiveness in various aspects of the business.

- Number, type, and difficulty of decisions made in management positions.
- Technical nature of the business, rate of growth, innovative nature, and changes inherent in its various aspects.
- Scope of the functional or operating segments for which the management position is responsible.
- Impact data such as sales, profits, net assets utilized, and number of employees.

Most of this information is, of course, readily available, for it is prepared for other purposes and can easily be put into a form which contributes to a successful management description program.

Adapting Job Evaluation Plans

Methods of job evaluation must also be adapted to the unique characteristics of the management-level job. Some of the factors used to evaluate clerical and production jobs, such as working conditions, physical effort, and visual concentration, have no application at the management level. And some factors which may not be pertinent to lower-level positions may measure the very essence of relative worth in management positions—for example, supervision exercised, relationships, know-how, and responsibility.

Frequently, too, the same factors have different meanings when applied to management and nonmanagement positions. "Responsibility" in a lower-level job, for example, may be interpreted primarily in terms of the cost of errors. Yet in management positions, responsibility is defined more in terms of scope of accountability and impact on the success of the business.

The complexity of management positions also affects the

type of evaluation plan utilized. Although the basic methods of evaluation illustrated back in Exhibit 4 are essentially the only ones available, many variations have been devised to adapt them to management levels. Simple ranking and classification systems have not been too helpful in measuring the value of management positions except in very small companies. This is because of the broad nature of management responsibilities and the variety of elements affecting job value. Point plans have also caused trouble when used alone, owing to the enormous difficulty of describing degrees of managerial responsibility and identifying factors which will differentiate meaningfully among the many types of management positions. Four adaptations which have had considerable success in management evaluation programs in recent years are the modified factor-comparison method, the multiple evaluation system, profiling, and the bench-marking system.

Modified factor comparison. The most direct application of that factor-comparison technique to management-level jobs requires the following modifications: (1) selection and definition of factors tailored to management jobs, (2) adaptation of weighting techniques, and (3) development of procedures which are geared to measuring management positions.

Factors selected must, of course, reflect the unique characteristics and responsibilities of management-level positions. In some cases, this has led to development of completely new factors; in others, it has meant modification or different emphases in definition. A difference in emphasis is illustrated in Exhibit 30, which is taken from a plan used by an electrical manufacturing company. The factor selected—know-how, in this case—is defined more in terms of the *types* of things which an evaluator should consider rather than in the specific and restrictive terms found in office and production plans.

The number of factors utilized may also be different in management positions. Experience indicates that no fewer than four or more than six factors are appropriate at this level. At least four factors are usually necessary to cover the basic criteria of responsibility, authority, knowledge, and management skills. But, if more than six are used, it almost invariably involves breaking down criteria so finely that they are more precise than the knowledge upon which judgments are based. It also commonly results in duplication, with more than one factor measuring the same characteristic.

The weighting techniques used in evaluating management-level positions are somewhat broader and more flexible than those suitable for office and production jobs. Predetermined weightings are almost impossible in man-

EXHIBIT 30
THE KNOW-HOW FACTOR

The amount of technical knowledge, understanding, judgment, intelligence, and similar qualities which an individual must have in order to accomplish the objectives and responsibilities of the job.

Consider such elements as:

- Amount of creative thinking and planning.
- Extent of decision making.
- Independence of thinking; extent to which problems must be solved without guidance or help from others.
- Number and diversity of subjects which must be understood.
- Comprehensiveness or intensity of understanding.
- Intangibles such as reasoning ability; forecasting skill; ability to identify cause, effect, and probable result; understanding of behavior, and so on.

agement positions, because the various factors differ greatly in importance from company to company. In the sales-oriented firm, for instance, the relationship factor will probably be dominant in determining relative job worth. On the other hand, in an engineering-oriented company, relationships may be less important than know-how.

Some companies have also found it extremely helpful to modify the format of the factor-comparison plan in order to focus attention upon some of the unique characteristics of management positions and to assist evaluators in gaining an overall view of the job-value decisions which they make. This is most often accomplished through the use of large guide charts which summarize the results of rankings under each factor.

Multiple evaluation. Another basic modification of the factor-comparison technique that is frequently used in management-level positions is simply to evaluate all jobs at least twice by different plans. When the results are compared, they pinpoint areas where one of the methods may be seriously inaccurate. In one widely used plan, for instance, all jobs are evaluated three times by defining overall job worth in three different ways: scope and impact of the job, requirements of the job, and difficulty of performing the job. Under each of these plans, factors are utilized. The results of the three evaluations are then compared; if any significant differences come to light, the jobs are rechecked to iron out the inconsistencies. While extremely costly, the approach recognizes the complexity of management-level position evaluation and helps to insure that the most important characteristics are adequately considered.

Profiling. Another common system is based on a different method of multiple evaluation. Instead of using more than one factor-comparison plan, the system calls for two different techniques. The first, illustrated under A of Exhibit 31, is a straight factor-comparison approach. The second, part B of Exhibit 31, is a process of internal evaluation which requires that each job be analyzed in terms of the relative importance of the three factors. The results of the two approaches, expressed in percentages, are compared, and any differences are resolved by re-evaluating the job by each method. Note that in the exhibit, the results of the evaluations of the foreman's job are inconsistent, so that re-evaluation will be necessary.

Bench marking. Some companies use direct salary-survey data and key-job comparisons to help establish proper pay relationships among management-level positions. One method calls for an identification of those management jobs within the company which are similar to positions reported in widely used surveys of management positions. Position evaluation begins with determination of the rela-

EXHIBIT 31

MULTIPLE EVALUATION IN THE PROFILE METHOD

A. Results of Factor Comparison

Job	Know-How Points	% of Total	Responsibility Points	% of Total	Relationships Points	% of Total
Foreman	20	24	25	29	40	47
Wage analyst	40	58	15	21	15	21
Salesman	25	23	35	32	50	45
Controller	50	36	50	36	40	28

B. Results of Profiling

Job	Know-How	Responsibility	Relationships
Foreman	30%	20%	50%
Wage analyst	60%	20%	20%
Salesman	20%	30%	50%
Controller	35%	35%	30%

tive values of these jobs according to the surveys. The relative values become the overall job evaluation points; these, in turn, are then profiled under each factor. The resulting market positions thus become the bench-mark positions against which all other management-level positions are compared.

There may be three types of bench-mark jobs. First are the senior executive positions, which have been established through direct survey from data filled in proxy statements of principal competitive companies. The second bench-mark source consists of those positions established in the highest level of nonmanagement groups, including supervisory, sales, and professional positions. The third bench-mark group involves special positions of particular pertinence or problem to the company, which are surveyed directly.

Management Salary Structure

In addition to the perplexing question of determining proper internal relationships among management jobs within the company, there are some unique problems in establishing the level of the salary structure—or in effect, setting proper external relationships. This has become a particularly important problem in recent years because of the intense competition for top management talent. In setting the salary structure for management personnel, the same basic techniques that have already been discussed can be utilized, although certain changes in emphasis may be necessary. Also, setting the management structure involves all the technical problems which have been outlined, as well as some special new complexities.

One of the traditional and frequently used methods is the company survey. The analysts select jobs and companies for survey, make direct comparisons, average the figures, and build a structure based upon the competitive information. For all but senior executive positions, this is an extremely difficult and costly method to use in setting the salary structure. (It should be noted, incidentally, that obtaining valid survey data is easiest at the very top and bottom of the salary structure. It becomes increasingly difficult toward the middle of the range. Middle management, senior sales, and senior professional jobs are the most difficult jobs of all to price.)

In surveying management-level positions, it is extremely difficult to select jobs for survey which occur in any significant number of competitive companies. One survey of middle management positions in the insurance industry, for instance, started with 35 survey jobs, but, on the average only 11 comparable positions were found in each of the surveyed companies. Also, it is difficult to draw comparisons even when descriptions are compared and personal visits are made to discuss each of the surveyed positions. This is due to the fact that most combinations of duties and responsibilities at the management level are somewhat unique to each company, even within the same industry.

Selecting the companies to survey also poses a problem. In general, management-pay surveys must be much broader in scope than surveys at lower job levels, since each company will report relatively few salaries for each job surveyed because of the individual nature of management positions. This, in turn, involves a second problem: Many companies do not like to give individual salary data on management positions, because they are identifying the salary of an individual. Still another complicating factor among management-level jobs is that the various management positions have separate labor markets. The competitive market for financial jobs may be quite different from the various competitive markets for manufacturing executives. Finally, each of the labor markets for management jobs is a national or at least a regional market.

All these considerations add so substantially to the cost of useful company surveys that few companies except the largest have the resources to undertake them. Most rely on published information about management compensation, among which the most widely used is that provided by the Executive Compensation Service of the American Management Association. Another source of data is the annual "Cost of Management Study," appearing in the January issue of *Business Management* magazine, which focuses on pay of top-level managers in more than 400 companies. Direct survey information for top-officer positions also can be obtained for specific companies from proxy statements. Finally, some industry associations and consulting firms publish special surveys of management compensation.

Salary structures covering management-level positions have some unique characteristics. For one thing, the within-grade progression is somewhat broader as a result of the greater importance of man worth over job worth in any management-level position. This in turn indicates the greater opportunity that exists for the individual to contribute on the job and provide significant motivation for management employees to improve their performance. Between-grade progressions are also larger in management structures because of the greater difficulty of classifying jobs into levels in the first place. At the same time, they are designed to maintain correct overlapping between grades.

In addition to their technical differences management salary structures differ from office and production structures in that they can be used only as broad guides for decision making. The results are simply not accurate enough to justify any rigid approach to administering salaries within the framework provided.

Salary Planning for Management Positions

The fact that job classification is more difficult and probably less precise among management positions than any others necessarily places greater emphasis on salary planning for the individual at this level. The difficulty of separating job worth from man worth in determining managers' compensation also suggests the importance of individual salary planning.

Faced with such difficult and complex decisions, line executives should certainly have basic information on each manager's pay history. They should also have data concerning pay comparisons within the company and pay levels outside the company. Finally, they should be given the opportunity to review this information in a systematic manner, and they should have staff personnel or higher-level managers available for counsel and guidance.

Among the factors which should be considered in determining a manager's pay progress are the results he achieves. Particularly in higher-level management positions, these are the primary determinants of a manager's worth. But since the typical manager may plan his own work, act independently to some extent, receive infrequent supervision, and have extensive relationships with the other managers throughout the company, judging results is not always a simple matter. The executive who is appraising such a manager frequently must rely on the judgments and reactions of other managers who deal with the man.

Another somewhat special consideration in management jobs is the greater focus on values as opposed to cost.

Although every dollar of cost is important, the potential benefit from increased values of management performance far outweighs the potential impact of higher payroll costs for managers. For example, one company noted that if it increased management payroll costs by 25 percent, it would reduce the after-tax return on net worth from 9.9 percent to 9.7 percent. Thus even a substantial increase in management compensation would result in an extremely small decrease in profit return. On the other hand, if the increase in compensation should attract higher-caliber people or should motivate existing management to perform more effectively, the result for the company might possibly be a 50 or 100 percent increase in rate of return.

There are also special pay-relations problems with management positions. The internal relationships among the salaries of executives in marketing, engineering, manufacturing, finance, and staff functions pose obvious difficulties. Where bonuses, stock options, and other forms of extra compensation are prevalent, the total compensation relationships, as well as base salary relationships, must be carefully administered.

Another important consideration in management positions is the proper differential reward for outstanding contributors. In any company, there is a relatively small number of truly outstanding individuals; it is not likely that more than 3 or 4 percent of the total management group will be thoroughly professional and endowed with outstanding capability and potential for future growth. It is doubtful, moreover, whether existing salary practices in most companies give adequate recognition to such outstanding persons. Is it enough to pay the truly exceptional man, the individual who is really carrying the burden of leadership within his group, who is solving major company problems, who holds in his hand the future of the organization, a 5, 10, or 15 percent increment over the average manager in the group? Would it not be more appropriate to pay him 30, 50, or even 100 percent more? This is one of the most perplexing pay-relationships problems faced by companies.

Salary Administration for Top Executives

These relatively few persons in the management group who are at the very apex of the company hierarchy require special consideration. It is just as difficult to define such executives as it is to define management generally. In general, they might be regarded as those managers who, by the nature of their judgments and decisions, affect the long-term achievements of the enterprise. These are usually persons whose salaries are personally reviewed by the board of directors. Probably they do not number more than one-fifth of 1 percent of the total employees of the company.

In addition to the elements of a formal salary administration program, there are special factors affecting pay decisions for executive management. Probably one of the most important concerns the income tax consequences for the individual executive. Another is the fact that the salaries of such executive managers set a ceiling under which the pay of all management employees and, indirectly, all employees throughout the company, must fall.

There are some guides which generally are considered in establishing the compensation for executive management. One is the size of the company: Various studies indicate that there is a definite relationship between the total compensation of the chief executive officer and company size. Another is the nature of the industry itself. While interindustry differentials are narrowing, there are still significant differences in the pay received by executives in companies of comparable size in different industries. Another very important factor is whether or not the chief executive officers, and executive management generally, receive a bonus. As a rule, salaries in bonus-paying companies are 10 to 20 percent lower than salaries in non-bonus-paying companies.

Incentive Compensation Plans

About 50 percent of all companies have some form of incentive compensation plan for management. These plans involve more than profit sharing or extra pay. Generally approved by stockholders, they provide for the setting aside, usually on a formula basis, of a proportion of the company's profits to pay bonuses to management. Until recently, only profit-making companies had such plans. Now, however, incentive compensation plans for nonprofit organizations have been devised.

Eligibility. To be truly an incentive compensation plan, a bonus arrangement should be restricted to managers. If managers are defined as those whose judgments and decisions have a significant impact on company profits, then a bonus plan geared to the profits should have an incentive value only for this management group. In practice, two-thirds of all profit-based bonus plans do restrict eligibility to management, and the number is increasing. Sometimes this involves providing nonmanagement personnel with other incentive compensation plans which have rewards geared to the expectations set for those positions.

There is also an increasing trend toward developing guides for determining individual eligibility. The experience of some companies has been that, in the absence of guides, additional positions tend to be admitted to the program each year. Because of the cumulative effect of such additions, either the bonus-fund formula must be unusually large so that an unreasonable proportion of profits goes to managers, or else the bonus for any manager becomes so small as to be uncompetitive.

Bonus-fund formulas. Bonus-fund formulas vary a great deal with economic and financial characteristics of different businesses. Most plans, however, prescribe first a deduction from profits and then a percentage above the deduction which may be accrued in the bonus fund. The deduction is set to provide a minimum target for management and also for the practical purpose of assuring adequate cash flow for the company.

True incentive compensation plans relate the bonus-fund formula to the financial goals of the business. In this way, there is incentive for achievement in bad business years as well as in good. Also, by gearing the fund to company goals, there is an increasing standard for management each year. This is the same incentive-compensation logic which has been applied to production-worker incentive plans for many years, but it has only recently been appearing in management incentive plans.

Individual payments. One of the most difficult aspects of a management incentive plan is to determine how to apportion the bonus fund to individuals. Although this has traditionally been at the discretion of top management, companies have had great difficulties with discretionary methods. Compensation committees of the board of directors do not usually know the jobs, the people, and their performance well enough to make intelligent decisions, so that they have increasingly urged senior management to establish guides for determining individual payments on an equitable basis. The key to the actual individual payments formula is found in the normal management practices of the enterprise. If, for instance, the standard management practice is to evaluate its managers through goal-setting techniques, then the same process can be used as one basis for determining the bonus received by individuals.

Amount and form of incentive payments. Exhibit 32 shows the average bonus payments in industry, expressed as a percent of base salaries. Note that high-level positions not only get higher bonuses but a higher percentage of bonus to salary. This is a logical reflection of the whole incentive-compensation purpose. Bonuses are to reward managers who affect profits by the nature of their positions; thus higher-level positions should have a higher percentage of their total compensation dependent upon the profit results of the business. Note also from Exhibit 32 that executives in bonus-paying companies receive

EXHIBIT 32
INCENTIVE COMPENSATION FOR MANAGERS:
TYPICAL INDUSTRY PAYMENTS
[$000 omitted]

Salary of Manager	Percent Bonus to Salary*	Total Compensation	Salary and Total Compensation in Non-Bonus-Paying Companies
$ 20	15	$ 23	$ 21
30	25	37	33
40	30	52	47
50	35	67	60
75	40	105	95
100	45	145	125
125	50	187	155
150	60	240	200
175	70	300	250
200	80	360	300

*Percent will be greater in years of high profits and lower, or zero, in years of poor profits.

more total compensation than their counterparts in non-bonus-paying companies. As a general rule, salaries of executives in non-bonus-paying companies are approximately 10 to 20 percent higher; but, since bonuses average 25 to 30 percent of salary, total compensation in bonus-paying companies tends to be about 15 percent higher than in firms which do not have bonus plans.

With respect to the form of bonus payments, companies may pay the bonus earned all in cash, all in the stock of the company, or some in cash and some in stock. In addition, the company may elect to pay the bonus over a number of years. The usual purpose of this is to set up a barrier to turnover, for such payments in future years commonly are contingent upon the executive's staying with the company. Finally, some companies permit executives to defer their bonus until retirement or termination of employment with the company. Frequently this is done through the establishment of a fund which will earn interest and be subject to capital gains.

Stock Options

Approximately one-third of all companies whose stock is traded on the New York or American Stock Exchange provide some form of stock-option grants for senior managers. This means that about 10 percent of executive management personnel receive supplemental income through a stock-option program. The income from these programs can represent a significant part of the total compensation of an executive.

Such plans have two special features. First, they are the only form of compensation which relates the future pay of executives to the long-range results of the operation; therefore, they are an eminently logical approach to compensation for executive positions. Second, if the stock-option plan is qualified, the income gain or the option profit will be taxed at capital-gains rates, so that the executive pays only one-half of his ordinary tax rate up to a maximum of 25 percent.

To qualify for capital-gains provisions, the stock-option plan must meet rather rigid tests. For one thing, capital gains applies only to that part of the option profit which is in excess of 100 percent of the price of the stock when the option was granted. Furthermore, the option must be held by the executive for a three-year period. In addition, no options can be exercised with capital-gains benefits so long as a preexisting option at a higher price is outstanding. Finally, option prices cannot be revalued, as was formerly the case. Some maintain that because of the tightening of stock option provisions which occurred a few years ago, this form of compensation is less attractive to executives than it was. The fact is, however, that in the time since the tax law changes, for every stock option plan which was abandoned there have been 20 adopted. Also, all evidence indicates that managers are exercising options at the same rate since the change as they did before.

The number of shares which are granted to executives under option plans varies a great deal. Typically, a company will reserve no more than 5 percent of total outstanding stock for purposes of issuing stock options. The amount of stock granted to any individual is normally a function of the job level; as in the case of bonus plans, the stock option values are a higher percentage of salary in higher-level jobs.

Exhibit 33 provides data on the multiple-of-earnings guide for granting stock options. In this widely used guide, the theory is that the price of stock under option multi-

EXHIBIT 33
Stock Option Plans: Typical Industry Grants and Option Income
[$000 omitted]

Salary of Executive	Multiple[1]	Percent of Annual Income[2]
$ 20	1.5	15
30	2.0	20
40	2.5	27
50	3.0	35
75	3.5	42
100	4.0	50
125	5.0	60
150	6.0	70
175	7.0	85
200	8.0	100

[1] Multiple equals price of stock at option multiplied by number of shares optioned divided by salary.
[2] Equals current price less option price multiplied by number of shares optioned divided by number of years, all expressed as a percent of salary. Actual value is, of course, a function of trend in the price of company stock.

plied by the number of shares optioned should represent a value which is a multiple of the executive's current salary. In the exhibit, the executive making $50,000 would have option grants for stock where the number of shares multiplied by the stocks would equal about $150,000; the $100,000 executive would have option values (price times a number of shares) equal to four times salary. Exhibit 33 also indicates the amount of income which may accrue to executives at various income levels from stock-option plans. The study of 37 companies used as a basis for the data was made during a period of rising stock prices. Under these ideal conditions, income from options was more than double that from incentive compensation plans. In some of the companies studied, stock option income was considerably greater than salary income.

Special Compensation for Executives

An important form of special compensation for some executives is deferred compensation. Under deferred-income plans, part of the income earned by an executive in a given year is literally deferred and paid to him at some future time, usually after retirement. The primary purpose of such plans is to postpone income to a year when the executive's tax rate is lower.

There are strict and complicated tax rules governing such deferred-compensation arrangements. Also, complex mathematics is need to determine whether or not a deferral is to the advantage of the executive. For instance, calculation of deferred compensation must take into consideration all the following factors: current income of the executive; total retirement income, including pensions and income from savings; likely changes in tax rates; and the income potential from after-tax income. These factors themselves involve a high degree of uncertainty. Determining the value of current after-tax income, for example, requires judgment as to interest rates and appreciation values from investments. Because of this uncertainty, deferred-compensation arrangements are prudent only if a considerable safety margin is built into them. As a general rule, executives who are within five years of retirement should earn at least $50,000 in total annual income before deferred-compensation arrangements will probably be to their advantage; executives who are ten years from retirement should earn well over $100,000 a year in order to make deferred arrangements practical.

There is also a wide variety of special benefits available to executives. For example, many companies have split-dollar insurance programs for their key men. Also, most companies allow longer vacations for executives. One recent study of 20 companies in the electronics industry, for example, showed that all of them provided four weeks of vacation or more for all executives, regardless of service. They also reported, however, that only 10 percent of the executives covered actually took the four-week vacation and 20 percent took no vacation at all.

Several types of fringe benefits for executives are usually not reported and are sometimes difficult either to identify or to assess. For instance, many companies provide periodic physical examinations for executives. A certain number of companies have special security agreements with executives to protect them against the possibility of discharge because of policy disagreements, changes in the nature of the business, or other factors beyond the control of the individual. Some of these arrangements are formalized in employment contracts; others are informal.

While in recent years the government has tightened up considerably on expense-account privileges for executives, a variety of legitimate business expense items certainly represents some value for executives. It is extremely difficult, of course, to assess such benefits; it is equally difficult to administer them. The same can be said for perquisites. Size of office, title, type of furniture, and other such status symbols have no real dollar value, but they may have a real value to the executive.

The bewildering array of forms of compensation for executives is one of the primary characteristics of management salary administration. Companies are constantly looking for new ways to reward managers for their contribution and to provide optimum motivation. The probability is, therefore, that there will be more forms of management compensation in the future, and that many of them will become increasingly complex. This poses technical problems for management itself. Essentially, it means that more and more companies will be focusing attention on the problems of management compensation.

CHAPTER XI

FRINGE BENEFITS AS ADDITIONAL COMPENSATION

IN ADDITION TO WAGES, EMPLOYEES—LIKE MANAGERS— receive compensation in the form of "fringe benefits." In essence, this term includes all employee income (and hence all company costs incurred directly on behalf of employees) beyond straight-time earnings. "Straight-time earnings" here means the employee's hourly rate for all the hours actually worked. Thus fringe benefits include the following:
- Insured benefits.
- Pay for time not worked.
- Premium or penalty payments.
- Legally required payments.
- Extra compensation.
- Employee services.

EXTENT OF FRINGE BENEFITS

"Fringe benefit" is really an unfortunate term to describe the variety of extra compensation usually extended to employees. Probably, when the term was first coined, the amount of these extra payments was so small that they really were fringe items. With the rapid growth of the various types in recent years and the substantial increase in the money involved, they have now become significant. Just how significant they are in terms of overall compensation is illustrated in Exhibit 34, which is based upon the actual wage costs of a leading machinery manufacturing company. This company paid 79 percent of its total payroll dollar in the form of wages and salaries and 21 percent in the form of fringe benefits. Of the 79 percent, it is estimated that only 60 percent was base pay; the other 19 percent represented extra pay under the firm's incentive compensation and profit-sharing plans. Thus employees

EXHIBIT 34
FRINGE BENEFITS IN THE WAGE DOLLAR

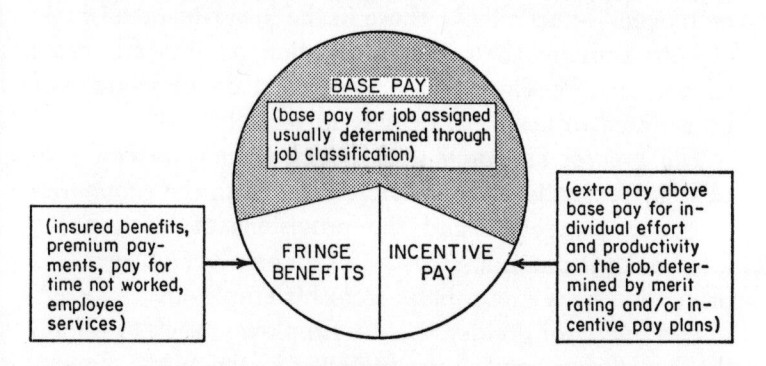

BASE PAY
(base pay for job assigned usually determined through job classification)

(insured benefits, premium payments, pay for time not worked, employee services) → FRINGE BENEFITS

INCENTIVE PAY ← (extra pay above base pay for individual effort and productivity on the job, determined by merit rating and/or incentive pay plans)

should recognize that fringe benefits are an important part of their pay, and employers should recognize that they are an important part of the cost of doing business.

Fringe benefits and wage payments complement each other, and both combined represent employee income and company wage costs. Increases in benefits are not, therefore, *supplemental* to wage increases; they are granted *in lieu of additional* wage increases. For example, a two-cent improvement in benefits must be regarded not as something granted in addition to, say, a six-cent increase but as an integral part of an eight-cent increase.

There is every indication that fringe benefits will continue to improve substantially in the future. Moreover, there are some very basic reasons why improvements have been sought in the past and will probably be sought in the future, even though they take the place of additional wage increases. Here are some of them.

The desire to meet, at least in part, the major economic risks faced by employees. The principal means of protection are: provision for retirement income, insurance against sickness or injury, and some guarantee against loss of income because of layoff or illness.

The fact that employers can provide for protection against these risks with greater certainty than individual employees. It would be difficult, if not impossible, for employees—particularly those in the lower-income brackets—to provide their own protection against all major economic risks. Even those who could do so would not be inclined to invest so heavily in security.

The greater economy with which employers can provide for protection against these risks. Both the economics of group protection and the provisions of existing tax laws make it much less costly for an employee to get this protection on a group basis from his employer.

The quest for greater leisure. Employees seek to obtain the benefits of greater productivity in the form of more leisure as well as in higher living standards. This is particularly true when living standards continually improve. The quest for more leisure manifests itself specifically in the demand for shorter hours of work, longer vacations, more rest periods, more holidays, and earlier retirement.

The cumulative effect of these benefits on a typical payroll can be seen in the summary of two industry surveys reproduced in Exhibit 35. Survey 1 was made of major electronic companies in the Middle Atlantic States area. The 23 companies surveyed paid an additional premium of 26 percent over straight-time earnings for the various fringe benefit items. The companies in survey 2 are all

EXHIBIT 35
Cost of Fringe Benefits

Benefit Item	Percentage of Average Base Pay	
	Area Survey 1	Area Survey 2
Pension	3.2	4.0
Other insured benefits	2.9	3.7
Premium payment	5.7	10.2
Pay for time not worked	8.8	10.1
Legally required payments	3.4	3.2
Extra compensation	1.6	2.1
Employee services	0.7	1.3
Total	26.3	34.6

large, nationally known firms. Here the benefit premium amounted to almost 35 percent.

CHECKLIST OF MAJOR FRINGE BENEFITS

Fringe-benefit administration is extremely complex—both because there are so many kinds of benefits and because many of the benefit items involve complicated insurance, legal, actuarial, or economic considerations. For this reason, specialists—either within the company or outside—are generally called upon to handle the technical ramifications of many fringe items. It is probably sufficient for the individual manager to be generally familiar with each item in the fringe package that affects income and costs and to understand the direct responsibilities he has in administering it. The following checklist of fringe benefits identifies the principal provisions in each case.

INSURED BENEFITS (financed and administered on a group insurance basis and basically geared to meeting major employee economic risks):

1. PENSION PLANS: Formal plans which provide income

for the worker after he retires. Key provisions generally include:

Membership requirements: Plan may be geared to minimum age, minimum service, or broad occupational group.

Benefit formula: Plans generally aim at benefits which give the retired worker one-third to one-half of his final earnings. Payment may be in the form of a flat amount, either including or excluding social security benefits; the amount may be geared to years of service or to both age and service. Frequently, a minimum benefit for those who meet the minimum eligibility requirements is also prescribed.

Retirement requirements: Generally plans call for retirement at age 65 with at least 15 years of service, but they may permit retirement as early as age 50 at a reduced benefit, or extended retirement with no additional benefits up to age 70 or 75.

Financing: A number of factors must be considered in the area of financing. Does the employee contribute to the cost of the plan? If so, how much does he contribute? Is the plan financed through a bank or insurance company, or is it pretty much on a "pay-as-you-go" basis?

2. HOSPITALIZATION BENEFITS: Insurance which provides for various hospital and medical expenses. Key provisions generally include:

Daily hospital payments: Full or partial payment of all the charges for hospital room and board for a specified number of days.

Extra charges: Prescribed payments for drugs, X-rays, and so forth.

Dependency coverage: The employee's family may be covered or not.

Financing: The amount of the employee's contribution toward the cost of his own coverage and that of his dependents.

3. SURGICAL BENEFITS: Frequently connected with the hospitalization benefits, surgical plans usually have prescribed payments providing for various types of operations or surgical treatment. As in the case of

hospitalization plans, it is important to determine whether or not dependents are covered, and how much the employee contributes to the cost of the plan.

4. MAJOR MEDICAL BENEFITS: Plans which provide for benefits in addition to those provided under the basic hospitalization and surgical plans. Key features generally include:
Eligibility: Some plans are restricted to certain groups of employees.
Corridor provisions: Frequently an employee must pay as much as $300 in charges over and above the hospitalization and surgical benefits before receiving benefits from the major medical plan.
Percentage payments: Plans usually pay up to 75 or 80 percent of actual charges.
Maximum payments: Maximum total payments equal to $5,000 or $10,000 per illness are usually specified.
Special features: Does the plan cover mental illness, travel, outpatient care, or other special expenses?
Dependency coverage: Are dependents covered for all types of illnesses?
Financing: Again, how much does the employee pay for his own coverage and that of his dependents?

5. LIFE INSURANCE: Regular or special group life insurance. Key provisions generally include:
Benefits schedule: Frequently benefits are geared to the annual earnings of the employee.
Supplemental benefits: Is there provision for double indemnity, disability benefits, continued life insurance coverage after retirement, and supplemental death benefits?
Financing: The amount and percent which the employee contributes.

6. SICKNESS AND ACCIDENT INSURANCE: Insured benefits paid directly to the employee to offset loss of income due to sickness or accidents. Key provisions generally include:
Benefits schedule: As in the case of life insurance, benefits

are frequently geared to the earnings of the employee.
Duration of benefits: Usually, these insured benefits last from 13 to 26 weeks.
Waiting period: There is frequently a waiting period of a week before an employee is eligible to collect benefits for sickness.
Financing: How much does the employee contribute?

7. DISABILITY PLANS (insured benefits paid for permanent disability for life of employee).

PAY FOR TIME NOT WORKED (various provisions which call for full pay to employees during periods when they are not actually working).

1. SICK LEAVE: Plans call for continuation of pay to employees absent from work owing to illness. Key provisions generally include:
   Amount of benefit: Some plans grant full pay even though income received from sick leave is not always counted as income for tax purposes. Others pay the difference between full pay and the benefits received from sickness and accident insurance.
   Duration of benefits: They may be limited to as little as one week per year, or they may continue for an indefinite period, particularly for high-rated executives.

2. VACATIONS: Key provisions generally include:
   Eligibility requirements: Plans specify the length of service required for vacations of one, two, three, or four weeks. Some also call for graduated vacations above those of one week's duration.
   Vacation pay: Some programs call for the employee to receive his regular base rate of pay while on vacation; others call for payment of average earnings.
   Pay for time worked during vacation shutdown: Plans frequently provide for an alternate vacation period, extra straight time, or time and a half for an employee working at company request during the regular vacation period.

Earned right: Some programs provide for accrued vacation pay, if an employee leaves.

3. HOLIDAYS: Key provisions generally include:
Number of paid holidays: This varies a great deal—generally from a minimum of 5 to as many as 13.
Provision for holidays which fall on a Saturday or Sunday: Frequently employees are given the following Monday when a holiday falls on a Sunday, and Friday when a holiday falls on a Saturday.
Premium pay for work on a regular holiday: Most companies provide for some premium payment to the employee who works on a holiday; the employee usually receives anywhere from half-time to time and a half in addition to the regular day's pay.

4. REST PERIODS: There may be either formal breaks at specified times during the day or informal time off the job for various personal reasons.

5. SEVERANCE PAY: This includes provisions for payment of lump sums to employees who are laid off. The amount of the benefit, when specified, is often geared to length of service.

6. SUPPLEMENTAL UNEMPLOYMENT PLANS: These plans, sometimes referred to as guaranteed annual wage plans, provide for partial-income payments to employees who are laid off for lack of work. Frequently they are integrated with the unemployment compensation benefits which an employee receives from the state. Key provisions generally include:
Benefit formula: This determines the amount of compensation, with or without unemployment compensation, which is paid to an employee.
Duration of benefits: This refers to the number of weeks during a layoff that an employee receives the benefits.
Financial arrangements: Employers are usually limited in their liability by the amount of money which they have set aside for this purpose.

Eligibility provisions: Often employees with extremely short service are excluded from these plans.

PENALTY PAYMENTS (various premium payments over and above base compensation, in addition to premium pay for work on holidays or vacations, which are allowed an employee primarily to make up for undesirable working conditions or for extended periods of work):

1. OVERTIME: Premium payments to an employee for work in excess of a prescribed number of hours per week. According to law, of course, an employer is required to pay time and a half for all work in excess of 40 hours per week except where the employee is specifically exempted. In some cases, double time is paid for excessive overtime, such as periods of work in in excess of 50 hours per week. In addition to the usual provision for payment of overtime, a more generous plan is frequently in effect which calls for the payment of overtime beyond eight hours per day and on Saturdays and Sundays, as such, regardless of the number of hours which have been worked during the week.
2. SHIFT DIFFERENTIALS: Premium payments may be made for each hour of work on night shifts, on either a cents-per-hour or a percentage basis.
3. HAZARD PAY: Generally these premiums take the form of special extra compensation during periods when the employee is exposed to unusually hazardous conditions.

LEGALLY REQUIRED PAYMENTS (financed in whole or in part by the employer, legally required by a state or federal government, and administered by government agencies):

1. SOCIAL SECURITY: The primary purpose of the Social

FRINGE BENEFITS

Security law, of course, is to provide retirement benefits at the age of 65 (reduced benefits at age 62), plus some death benefits and disability provisions. Provisions now cover medical care for the elderly as well.

2. WORKMEN'S COMPENSATION: State laws customarily require lump-sum disability payments, indemnity payments for loss of earnings, and payment of medical expenses to an employee injured on the job.
3. UNEMPLOYMENT COMPENSATION: State agencies make direct payments to employees during periods of unemployment. The amount and duration of the benefits vary considerably among the states.

EXTRA COMPENSATION (various types of benefit plans which provide the employee with earnings in addition to regular base and premium compensation which they receive):

1. PROFIT SHARING: Predetermined plans which call for distribution of part of the company's profits to employees at periodic intervals and according to a prescribed formula. Profit sharing is usually restricted to the higher-level management employees.
2. BONUSES: Generally, bonuses differ from profit-sharing plans in that there is no fixed basis for paying these extra sums to employees. They may take the form of year-end Christmas gifts, or they may be arbitrary payments to selected employees.
3. SAVINGS PLANS: Savings plans for the worker under which the employer contributes cash or company stock to the employee's savings account. Usually the employer's contribution is directly proportional either to the employee's compensation or to the amount the employee puts into the savings plan.
4. SUGGESTION SYSTEMS: Programs which reimburse em-

ployees for ideas or suggestions which contribute to a more efficient and profitable business operation. Generally the suggestions are reviewed by management committees which attempt to set a value on each suggestion.

5. EXPENSE ACCOUNTS: Expense-account privileges accorded to an employee may actually represent significant extra compensation.

EMPLOYEE SERVICES (various services, privileges, and activities extended to an employee).

1. EMPLOYEE ACTIVITIES: Employers have, of course, sponsored many forms of employee activities including sports, social events, company recreation areas, and so on. The cost of these activities can be substantial to a company.
2. CAFETERIA: Many corporations subsidize the food-catering services provided to the worker during lunch and rest periods.
3. DISCOUNT PURCHASE: Most companies give employees the privilege of purchasing company products at a discount.
4. MEDICAL SERVICES: Frequently company dispensaries provide emergency medical treatment. In addition, some companies pay for X-rays, polio shots, and so forth.

ADMINISTRATION OF FRINGE BENEFITS

Although this checklist presents only the barest outline of fringe benefits, it does indicate the principal items, and it should help the individual supervisor analyze the benefits in effect at his own company. Beyond this, he must, of course, have a good working knowledge of his company's plans in order to meet his responsibility for administering the various benefits and for explaining them to employees.

Informing Employees About Benefits

Without expert specialized knowledge in the various benefit areas, it would be unreasonable to expect the manager to be able to provide complete and detailed information to employees regarding fringe benefits. As a result, the supervisor can be responsible only for outlining the broader aspects of the benefit program.

Information about the program is usually communicated in a number of ways, owing to the diversity and complexity of the benefits offered. In most companies, booklets describing key items, particularly those insured, are prepared and distributed to employees. Policy books provide data on other benefits. Merely putting such information in written form does not, of course, communicate it to employees. It provides only a written reference for those who choose to read. If the manager really wants his employees to know what their fringe compensation is, he must take more affirmative steps. As a result, companies frequently have personnel or insurance specialists explain various aspects of the benefit program to employees in group meetings and publish special announcements about them in company publications or on company bulletin boards.

When specific questions arise, the supervisor must make sure that the employee understands what provisions are in effect and what their value is to the employee. The worker, for instance, who finds himself with a hospital bill suddenly becomes acutely concerned with the hospitalization benefits provided by the employer. It is at this time that the supervisor has the best opportunity to make sure that the employee understands their full value. If a proper explanation is given under these conditions, he will gain a genuine understanding and appreciation of the benefits which are provided. Similar opportunities occur whenever overtime compensation, vacations, holidays, and other fringe benefits actually affect individual employees in their day-to-day work.

To answer some questions, particularly those involving more technical matters, the supervisor will probably have to refer employees to a personnel specialist or to an insurance counselor. Even here the supervisor can follow up to make sure that the counselors are providing the information and clear explanation that are necessary in each case.

Handling Controversial Issues

In informing employees about benefits, managers frequently encounter grievances over benefits or become involved in some of the more controversial questions relating to them. Probably the most important of these controversial issues is how the company's benefits compare with those of other companies in the area or in the industry. Such comparisons are extremely difficult to make even under ideal conditions because of the many kinds of benefits which are in effect and because of the complexity of some of the provisions.

When a comparison is undertaken, the most important thing is for the manager to avoid the tendency to judge the overall program on the basis of one specific provision. Even companies which have outstanding benefit plans may not, and probably will not, have the best to offer in every category. It is possible, for instance, that the company with the best benefit program in the country may have a less liberal hospitalization plan than some other company. For this reason, it is extremely important for both employees and managers to regard benefits in terms of "packages." The format of benefits, and the provisions on which company and employees place the principal emphasis, may merely reflect collective bargaining demands, industry practices, peculiarities in the company's operations, or employee preferences.

Employees do not always realize the cost of fringe benefits. Some items, such as rest periods, tend to be viewed as very small. As a result, when the supervisor enforces the limits on rest periods, employees may consider him guilty of pinchpenny tactics. The fact of the matter is that rest periods can be a large cost item. Furthermore, unless the official rest periods are enforced, inconsistent treatment of employees may arise or, through gradual relaxation of control, the number and cost of rest periods may easily become excessive, impairing the company's ability to grant other improvements in wages and benefits. For this reason, it is good to have some idea of the cost of each of the items in the benefit package and be in a position to explain it to employees in specific cases.

Another controversial issue, which is of particular interest to employees, is why they are required to contribute to the cost of some of the fringe benefits. A good case can be built up for either the contributory or the noncontributory approach to benefit financing. One of the principal arguments in favor of the contributory approach is that, by taking part in the cost of benefits, employees will have a greater appreciation of their value. While this argument may or may not have validity, it certainly makes no great impression on employees. A more significant reason from the employee's point of view is the fact that the company, at any given time, is able to finance just so much in wages and benefits. By contributing to the cost of the benefits, the employee is, in effect, making broader protection possible.

Preventing Abuses

With a few notable exceptions, employee benefits are applied automatically. That is to say, all employees receive fixed benefits according to predetermined provisions. The program is to this extent either self-supervised or administered by some central office of the company or by an insurance carrier. The exceptions, however, can be extremely significant and costly.

Such items as pensions, hospitalization, surgical benefits, life insurance, sickness and accident insurance, vacations, and holidays do not present problems of administration to the supervisor. In each instance, the eligibility of employees is fairly fixed, and the benefits which they receive are well prescribed. This is not the case, however, with sick leave, rest periods, overtime compensation, and similar benefits.

Sick leave, for example, is easily abused to the point where it becomes merely a supplementary paid vacation for employees, whether they are sick or not. All the elaborate controls in the world cannot administer it effectively—this is one area which is strictly the responsibility of the individual supervisor. Much the same can be said about rest periods; even misuse in small amounts can result in significant costs by the end of the year. Again, only the supervisor is in a position to administer the rest-period provisions and make sure that employees do not abuse their privileges.

Finally, there is the question of overtime. On frequent

occasions, of course, overtime work may be required by operations or may be economically justified. However, employees frequently look to overtime merely as a means of increasing their total income. In addition, as they become accustomed to working overtime regularly, they come to regard the extra income as part of their fixed income and begin to count on it. When overtime becomes a regular practice, it is doubtful whether the company is getting the additional amount of work which should result from the extra hours that employees put in on a job. Some studies have indicated that employees tend to spread out work to require overtime unless supervisors administer the provisions of overtime work with great care.

Impact of Benefits on Compensation

These benefit provisions not only affect the amount of compensation an employee receives but also to a significant extent determine the format of that compensation and the total pay relationships among different employees. Some benefits tend to flatten the total compensation picture—for example, sickness and accident benefits that call for flat monthly payments or a progressive schedule which is not in direct relationship to compensation. Other benefits, such as vacations, emphasize length of service with the company as opposed to performance on the job. This means that employees with longer service tend to receive more favorable treatment than employees with shorter service, regardless of income level or the job to which they have been assigned. To the extent that these provisions affect employee attitudes, they therefore constitute a direct incentive for staying with the company a longer period of time and no direct incentive for improving job performance or operating more effectively.

Again, benefit income is largely nontaxable income, a fact which also affects total compensation relationships. The general effect is, of course, a narrowing one, with all that this implies in terms of rewarding and motivating workers.

Obviously, then, benefits affect the very nature of employee compensation and company wage costs. Largely because of the variety of problems and objectives which underlie the adoption of benefits, the benefit package contains many different items, some of which are highly complex. This, in turn, leads to extreme complexities for the supervisor in communication and administration. Nevertheless, the amounts involved are ample evidence that facing and solving these problems is an essential part of the wage and salary responsibility of the individual manager.

THE INDIVIDUAL MANAGER'S RESPONSIBILITIES

THE SPECIAL ADMINISTRATIVE DIFFICULTIES WHICH HAVE been discussed, combined with the limitations of wage and salary administration noted earlier, all point up one basic fact: In spite of the laws, ground rules, controls, techniques, and programs which have been developed to guide supervisors in their pay decisions, the fundamental instrument of wage and salary administration is still *management judgment*. The various aspects of a formal wage and salary program are directed toward improving that judgment—which, ideally, will be based on the facts and circumstances relating to each pay problem.

The quality of a manager's pay decisions will improve when he understands the basic objectives of wage and salary administration and his responsibilities within the program. It will improve when he gains sufficient knowhow in the area so that he can apply the various principles which have been tested both technically and practically. Finally, of course, there is the basic question of motivation. The manager must come to recognize its importance to all involved. He must develop the desire to make decisions which genuinely solve pay problems in a way to attain the best balance among the interests of owners, managers, and employees.

These responsibilities together represent a tall order

for managers. If we were to translate generalities into specific assignments for the typical line manager, we would come up with a "job description of wage and salary administration responsibilities," such as that in Exhibit 36.

EXHIBIT 36
JOB DESCRIPTION
WAGE AND SALARY RESPONSIBILITIES OF THE
LINE MANAGER

The line manager is responsible for carrying out the pay program of the company within the framework of established company compensation policies and practices. Specifically, he will—

1. Review all job descriptions to make sure that they represent the most efficient and economic distribution of job duties, that each job assignment listed is essential to the basic functioning of the organizational unit, and that the descriptions are accurate statements of duties actually assigned and performed.
2. Report all changes in assignments to make sure that descriptions are current.
3. Review all job evaluation determinations for accuracy.
4. Effectively recommend pay increases of all types on the basis of the facts and equities of each case and within the framework of existing policy.
5. Carefully review work methods and work standards, where applicable.
6. Administer the wage incentive program, where applicable.
7. Control overtime work by determining the need for it, assure the equitable distribution of overtime assignments among employees, and review the effect of overtime work on gross pay relationships throughout the company.
8. Insure that employees get the full value of the fringe benefits provided.
9. Administer benefit programs and control abuses.

10. Report compensation needs and problems to appropriate levels of management.
11. Communicate all aspects of the compensation program to subordinates. This includes answering questions and handling complaints.
12. Insure compliance with applicable state and Federal compensation laws.
13. Insure compliance with union contract provisions.
14. Review and audit compensation decisions of subordinates as appropriate.

This is an impressive list, implying a broad understanding of wage and salary administration plus a detailed knowledge of the company's policies, programs, and practices.

How does the manager fulfill all these obligations in the face of operating pressures? Even the most enthusiastic advocate of sound wage and salary administration must recognize that the line executive is limited in the time he can give to such duties. For one thing, he has equal responsibility for other aspects of a balanced personnel program, such as employment and training. Furthermore, he must devote some time to his line responsibilities. As a result, the typical manager can probably spend little more than one hour per week on wage and salary matters.

This limited time means that the wage and salary program should be devoid of frills. In addition, it means that line personnel should be relieved of as much of the record-keeping and other routine aspects of wage and salary administration as possible. Finally, it means that the line manager cannot function all alone; he needs help. He can be given this help in two ways: First, he needs a sound wage and salary program, one that will genuinely back him up in meeting his responsibilities. Second, he needs the support of thoroughly qualified, professionally trained personnel people who can bring competent technical knowledge to bear on the important task of helping him solve the pay problems of the business.

INDEX

Administrative employees, compensation of, 202–204
    defined, 202–204
Antidiscrimination laws, 116–117
Appraisal of performance, as distinguished from merit rating, 82, 87, 88, 97–101
Approval, management, of wages and salaries, 135–136
Auditing, of sales compensation program, 174–175
    of wage and salary program, 30
Automatic approach to individual pay determination, 80–82

Bargaining on wages and salaries, collective, 22–23
    individual, 22, 184
    laws governing, 117–119
Base pay (for salesmen), determination of, 167–170
    versus incentive, 164–165
Bench-marking, as an aid in management compensation, 215–216
Bonuses, 239
    for management, 222–225
    for professionals, 189
    for salesmen, 171
    for supervisors, 199–200
Budgetary control of wages and salaries, 132–134
Business Management magazine, annual "Cost of Management Study," 218

Cafeteria, company, 240
Career compensation, 138–140
Career-curve approach to classifying professional employees, 181–184
Checklist, for merit rating, 85–86
Classification system of job evaluation, 42–43
Collective bargaining, 22–23, 110
    laws governing, 117–119
Commission plans, 170–171
Communication with employees, on fringe benefits, 241–244
    on incentives, 158, 173–174
    on job evaluation, 39, 56–60
    on merit rating, 107–109

INDEX

    on the pay structure, 75–77
    on wage and salary policies, 115
Control, of the wage and salary program, 131–137
    budgetary, 132–134
    by approval, 135–136
    by influence, 136–137
    statistical, 134–135
Counseling, as aid in salary planning, 104–105
    to improve merit rating skills, 91–92
Critical incident method of merit rating, 87

Deferred compensation, 228
Demotion, 127–128
Disability insurance plans, 236
Discipline, 157–158
Discount purchases, 240
Downgrading, 127

Employee activities, 240
Employees' questions, on incentives, 158
    on job evaluation, 56–60
Evaluation, of jobs, 31–60
    of performance, *See* Merit rating
    of specific positions, *See* Job evaluation
Executive Compensation Service, American Management Association, 165, 186, 218
Expense accounts, 240
    for management personnel, 229

Factor-comparison system of job evaluation, 45–46
    modified for management-level jobs, 212–214
Fair Labor Standards Act, 116, 201
Formal wage and salary program, elements of, 24
    need for, 21–23
Fringe benefits, considered as extra compensation, 230–246
    for executives, 229
    for professionals, 189–190
Functional approach to describing professional positions, 177–178

General pay increases, 142–143
Generic approach, to classifying professional employees, 180–181
    describing professional positions, 178–179
Geographic differences in pay levels, 141
Goal setting, as a basis for determining individual pay, 88–89
Gold-circle situations, 130
Green-circle situations, 130
Grievance system, union, 119
Ground rules for pay administration, 119–131
Group incentive systems, 147–148
Grouping, as merit rating technique, 85–86

Guaranteed annual wage. *See* Supplemental unemployment plans
Guaranteed work standards, 153–154

Halsey gain-share plan, 147
Hazard pay, 238
Hiring rates, 119–121
Holidays, 237–238
Hospitalization benefits, 234

Incentive plans, compensation,
    for supervisors, 199–200
    for managers, 222–225
    for salesmen, 170–172
    wage, *See* Wage incentive plans
Increases, re-evaluation or inequity, 128–129
    merit, 121–124
    promotional, 124–126
    general, 142–143
"Incremental compensation plan," 172–173
Individual bargaining, 22, 184
Individual contribution approach to evaluating professional positions, 184–185
Individual pay determination, 78–109
    automatic approach, 80–82
    informal approach, 79–80
    single rate approach, 79
Inequity increase, 128–129
Influence, control of wages and salaries by, 136–137
Informal approach to individual pay determination, 79–80
Insurance, life, 235
    sickness and accident, 235–236
    See also Hospitalization; Surgical Benefits; Disability Plans; Major Medical Benefits; Pension Plans
Integration of pay structures, 186, 206–207
Interface problems. *See* Pay relationships, within a particular company
Inventory, manpower, 100–101
    merit rating, 83–85

"Job," defined, 33
Job descriptions, 36–39
    use of, by management, 37–39
Job duties, analysis of, 32–36
    description of, at management level, 207–211
    professional, 177–179
    sales, 163
    supervisors, 192–193
    technical, 201
Job evaluation, 31–60
    of management positions, 211–216

INDEX

    of professional positions, 179–185
    of sales positions, 168, 169
    of supervisory positions, 192–193
    of technical positions, 201, 202
Job specifications, 36–37
Job titling, 179

Legally required payments, 238–239
Legislation on wages and salaries, 115–117
Life insurance, 235
Line manager, wage and salary functions of, 28–29, 54–60, 107–109, 122, 123, 125, 156–159, 241–245, 247–249
"Lump sum" merit increase, 122

Major medical benefits, 235
Management-level jobs, description of, 207–211
    compared to office and production jobs, 209
Management opportunities in pay administration, 17–30
Management personnel, compensation of, 216–229
Management positions, defined, 205–206
Manpower inventory, 100–101
"Market approach" to wage and salary administration, 22
Maximums, pay, 73–74
Medical benefits. *See* Hospitalization; Major medical benefits; Surgical benefits
Medical services, 240
Merit increases, amount of, 121–123
    frequency of, 123–124
Merit rating, 82–109
    problems of, 92–96
    techniques, *See* Graphic rating scales; Checklists; Grouping and ranking; Critical incident method; Standards of performance; Goal setting; Appraisal
Methods, work, 154–157
Minimums, pay, 72
    legal requirements, 116
Motivation, of workers, 151, 157–158
    of professionals, 188
Multiple evaluation, 90, 214–215

National Labor Relations Act, 117
Needs, company, identification of, 25

Objectives in wage and salary administration, determination of, 25–26
Office vs. hourly paid employees, 138
Overtime pay, 116, 238, 244–245
    for supervisors, 196–199
    for technical employees, 201

Pay administration, management, cost of, 144
    ground rules for, 119–131
    opportunities in, 17–30
Pay grades, establishment of, 61–77
    factors affecting, on supervisory level, 193–194
    on professional level, 179–185
    for salesmen, 167–169
    techniques, 62–65
Pay policy, company, 70–72, 111–115
Pay problems, 13–30
Pay relationships, among different companies, 18–19, 75, 221–222
    in different geographical areas, 141
        within a particular company, 18, 72–75, 138, 155, 194, 195, 196, 198, 199, 201, 220, 245–246
Pay structure. *See* Salary structure
Penalty payments, 238
Pension plans, 233–234
Performance, standards, 87–88
    appraisal of, *See* Appraisal of performance
Physical examinations, 229
Piecework incentive plan, 146–147
Planned compensation arrangements (for salesmen), 172
Point evaluation system of job evaluation, 43–44
Point incentive wage systems, 147
"Post-merit rating interview," 108
Prejudice in merit rating, avoidance of, 91
Preplanning of pay increases, 104–107
    for salesmen, 172
    See also Budgetary controls of pay increases
Pricing of jobs, 61–77
    professional, 185–188
    supervisory, 193–195
Professional employees, classification of, 180–181
Professional jobs, defined, 176–177
Professional personnel, compensation of, 176–190
Profiling (in job evaluation), 214–215
Profit sharing. *See* Bonuses
Program, wage and salary, planning and administration of, 26–27, 110–144
Promotional increases, 124–126

Questions, employees', on incentives, 158
    on job evaluation, 56–60
Quota system (in salesmen's compensation), 171

Ranking, as merit rating technique, 85, 87
Ranking system of job evaluation, 41–42
Rating scales, graphic (for performance evaluation), 83–85
Rating system. *See* Classification system of job evaluation
Red-circle situations, 129

INDEX

Re-evaluation, increase, 128–129
Responsibility, for wage and salary administration, 27–30
    of staff, 29–30, 91–92
    See also Line manager, wage and salary functions of
Rest periods, 237, 243, 244
Retirement benefits. *See* Pension plans
Review, of performance, 99–101

Salary planning, 103–109
    for management, 219–221
Salary structure, integration of, 186, 206–207
    for management personnel, 216–219
    for professional employees, 185–188
    traditional, 68, 72–75
Sales job, defined, 160–161
Salesmen, non-supervisory, compensation of, 160–175
Savings plans, 239
Scales, rating (for performance evaluation), 83–85
Severance pay, 237
Shift differentials, 238
Sick leave, 236, 244
Sickness and accident insurance, 235–236
Silver-circle situations, 131
Single rate approach to determination of individual pay, 79
Social security payments, 238–239
Special compensation, for executives, 228–229
    for professionals, 189–190
    for salesmen, 169–170
Staff responsibility for wage and salary administration, 29–30, 91–92
Standard-hour incentive plan, 147
Standard job evaluation approach to classifying professional employees, 180
Standards, performance, 87–88
    work, 148–149, 153–154, 156–158
Statistical control of wage and salary administration, 134–135
Stock option plans, 225–227
Subprofessional employees, 200
Suggestion systems, 239–240
Supervisor, defined, 192
Supervisory personnel, compensation of, 191–200
Supplemental unemployment plans, 237–238
Surgical benefits, 234–235
Survey, wage, 66–69
    management-pay, 216–218
    professional pay, 185–186

Taylor, Frederick W., differential-piece-rate plan, 147
Technical employees, defined, 200
Technical personnel, compensation of, 200–202

Top executives, defined, 221
    salary administration for, 221–222

Unemployment Compensation, 239
Union attitudes toward wage and salary administration, 117–119
U.S. Bureau of Labor Statistics, 186
Unsatisfactory performance, demotion for, 128
Upgrading, 126–127
    of technical jobs, 202

Vacations, 236–237
    for executives, 228–229

Wage and salary administration. *See* Pay administration
Wage and salary policies, company, 111–115
Wage and salary program, importance of, 17–18
    planning and administration of, 26–27, 103–109, 110–144
Wage incentive plans, 145–159
Walsh-Healey Act, 116
"Whipsawing," 119
Workmen's Compensation, 239
Work methods, 154–157
Work standards, 156–158
    determination of, 148–149
    guaranteed, 153–154

HD
4909
.S52
1967
(1)

SIBSON, Robert Earl
  Wages and Salaries

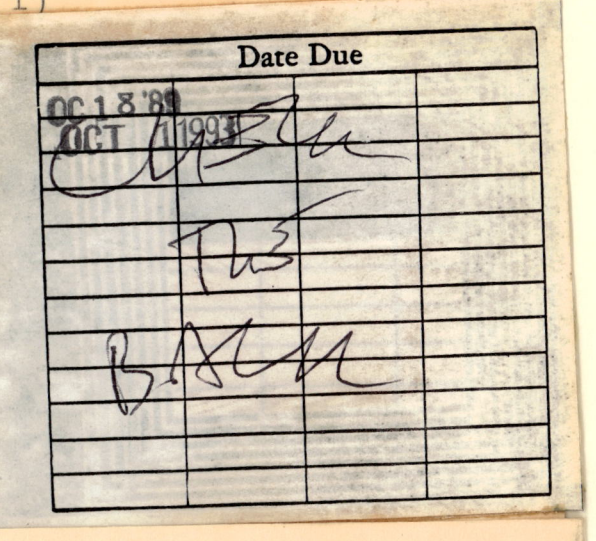

Date Due

OC 18 '89
OCT 1 1993

THE COMMUNITY COLLEGE OF ALLEGHENY COUNTY
ALLEGHENY CAMPUS
808 RIDGE AVENUE
PITTSBURGH, PA.
15212
LIBRARY

VOID

PRINTED IN U.S.A.